Spiritual
Healing
for Personal
Prosperity

Spiritual Healing for Personal Prosperity

By Edgar Cayce

A.R.E. Press • Virginia Beach • Virginia

A.R.E. Press
215 67th Street
Virginia Beach, VA 23451–2061

ISBN 13: 978–0–87604–609–8 (trade pbk.)

Cover design by Richard Boyle

Contents

Foreword
Who Was Edgar Cayce?

Edgar Cayce (1877–1945) has been called "the Sleeping Prophet," "the father of holistic medicine," "the miracle man of Virginia Beach," and "the most documented psychic of all time." For forty-three years of his adult life, he had the ability to put himself into some kind of self-induced sleep state by lying down on a couch, closing his eyes, and folding his hands over his stomach. This state of relaxation and meditation enabled him to place his mind in contact with all time and space and gave him the ability to respond to any question he was asked. His responses came to be called "readings" and contain insights so valuable that even to this day Edgar Cayce's work is known throughout the world. Hundreds of books have explored his amazing psychic gift, and the entire range of Cayce material is accessed by tens of thousands of people daily via the Internet.

Although the vast majority of the Cayce material deals with health and every manner of illness, countless topics were explored by Cayce's psychic talent: dreams, philosophy, intuition, business advice, the Bible, education, childrearing, ancient civilizations, personal spirituality, improving human relationships, and much more. In fact, during Cayce's lifetime, he discussed an amazing 10,000 different subjects!

The Cayce legacy presents a body of information so valuable that Edgar Cayce himself might have hesitated to predict its impact on contemporary society. Who could have known that eventually terms such as meditation, auras, spiritual growth, reincarnation, and holism would become household words to millions? Edgar Cayce's A.R.E. (the Association for Research and Enlightenment, Inc.) has grown from its humble beginnings to an association with Edgar Cayce Centers in countries around the world. Today, the Cayce organizations consist of hundreds of educational activities and outreach programs, children's camps, a multi-million-dollar publishing company, membership benefits and services, volunteer contacts and programs worldwide, massage and health services, prison and prayer outreach programs, conferences and workshops, and affiliated schools (Atlantic University: AtlanticUniv.edu and the Cayce/Reilly School of Massotherapy: EdgarCayce.org/massageschool).

Edgar Cayce was born and reared on a farm near Hopkinsville, Kentucky. He had a normal childhood in many respects. However, he could see the glowing energy patterns that surround individuals. At a very early age he also told his parents that he could see and talk with his grandfather—who was deceased. Later, he developed the ability to sleep on his schoolbooks and retain a photographic memory of their entire contents.

As the years passed, he met and fell in love with Gertrude Evans, who would become his wife. Shortly thereafter, he developed a paralysis of the vocal cords and could scarcely speak above a whisper. Everything was tried, but no physician was able to locate a cause. The laryngitis persisted for months. As a last resort, hypnosis was tried. Cayce put himself to sleep and was asked by a specialist to describe the problem. While asleep he spoke normally, diagnosing the ailment and prescribing a simple treatment. After the recommendations were followed, Edgar Cayce could speak normally for the first time in almost a year! The date of that first reading was March 31, 1901.

When others discovered what had happened, many began to seek help. It was soon learned that Edgar Cayce could put himself into this unconscious state and give readings for anyone—regardless of where the person was. If the advice was followed, he or she got well. Newspapers throughout the country carried articles about Cayce's work, but it wasn't really until Gertrude was stricken with tuberculosis that the power of the readings was brought home to him. Even with medical treatments she continued to grow worse and was not expected to live. Finally, the doctors said there was nothing more they could do. Cayce gave a reading that contained a recommendation for osteopathy, inhalants, enemas, dietary changes, and prescription medication. The advice was followed, and Gertrude returned to perfectly normal health!

For decades, the Cayce readings have stood the test of time, research, and extensive study. Further details of Cayce's life and work are explored in such classic books as *There is a River* (1942) by Thomas Sugrue, *The Sleeping Prophet* (1967) by Jess Stearn, *Many Mansions* (1950) by Gina Cerminara, and *Edgar Cayce: An American Prophet* (2000) by Sidney Kirkpatrick. Further information about Edgar Cayce's A.R.E., as well as activities, materials and services, is available at <u>EdgarCayce.org</u>.

Throughout his life, Edgar Cayce claimed no special abilities, nor did he ever consider himself to be some kind of twentieth-century prophet. The readings never offered a set of beliefs that had to be embraced, but instead focused on the fact that each person should test in his or her own life the principles presented. Though Cayce himself was a Christian and read the Bible from cover to cover every year of his life, his work was one that stressed the importance of comparative study among belief systems all over the world. The underlying principle of the readings is the oneness of all life—a tolerance for all people and a compassion and understanding for every major religion in the world.

Edgar Cayce on Dealing with Personal Financial Problems

Considering the fact that Edgar Cayce lived during a time of global uncertainty, the Great Depression, personal and economic hardship, and the world at war, it may not be surprising to learn that nearly 200 of Cayce's psychic readings mention the topic of personal financial problems and economic healing. People from every imaginable background and occupation came to him seeking answers to questions about their health, their personal challenges, their family situation, their careers, their direction in life, and their finances. The information they received continues to be helpful—studied by individuals the world over—as Cayce's insights for every imaginable issue and personal problem remain just as relevant today.

What may be surprising is that the information in the Cayce files on personal financial problems is about much more than money. Ultimately, material gains cannot be an end unto themselves. Instead, Cayce's premise is that any economic challenge faced by an individual is inextricably connected to a personal lesson or an opportunity to apply spiritual or universal laws in everyday life. Rather than seeing financial hardships as some sort of punishment or mistakenly assuming that the experience of poverty can somehow make someone more spiritual, the Cayce readings suggest that—seen correctly—the process of achieving economic healing can embody a worthwhile experience in personal growth.

Ultimately, everything we think we possess is in fact lent to us by God for the purpose of stewardship and service. Forgetting or ignoring or remaining ignorant of this premise is frequently one of the reasons that we encounter challenges in our personal finances. However, it is not that we are asked to give away everything we have. Instead, we are encouraged to become cognizant of the fact that personal success is best measured in terms of how we use our success to assist others. In terms of giving money away, Cayce specifically recommended giving a tithe of ten percent to charity, service activities, or to an individual in need.

Another issue that sometimes leads to financial lack is fear. Whether fear of the future, fear of monetary problems, or fear of situations that arise from personal challenges—such as the loss of a job—all of these things can work contrary to the flow of universal abundance. In the case of fear, Edgar Cayce often encouraged individuals to have faith and to use what they had in hand in order to draw to themselves additional opportunities and financial assistance. He often reminded individuals of economic healing principles from scripture, including Matthew 6:28–33, which is not an encouragement to sit idle and do nothing but rather an admonition to make certain one's focus is in the appropriate direction:

> Consider the lilies of the field, how they grow; they toil not, neither do they spin . . .
>
> Wherefore, if God so clothe the grass of the field, which today is, and tomorrow is cast into the oven, shall he not much more clothe you, O ye of little faith?
>
> Therefore take no thought, saying, What shall we eat? or, What shall we drink? or, Wherewithal shall we be clothed?
>
> . . . for your heavenly Father knoweth that ye have need of all these things.
>
> But seek ye first the kingdom of God, and his righteousness; and all these things shall be added unto you.

In addition to overcoming fear, cultivating faith, using what you have in hand, and practicing stewardship and personal tithing, the readings provide a number of suggestions for improving financial well-being. These include working with spiritual ideals, becoming cognizant of personal lessons needed by the soul (and attempting to learn them), living your soul's purpose, and being of service to others.

During the 1940s, a group of Cayce enthusiasts from New York City began working with various concepts from the Cayce readings and universal laws in an attempt to overcome the financial challenges that each of the individuals had been experiencing. Members of the group immediately recognized that their own economic problems were not linked to a lack of talent or potential but instead to other factors. For that reason, group members chose to begin applying spiritual principles to their material lives, while removing any of their own mental blocks regarding the challenges with their own finances.

The group began working as essentially an economic healing support group and undertook a three-month program of prayer, meditation, working with spiritual principles, and improving attitudes and their relationships with others, as well as tithing money and time. Although the group was small and not all of the individuals in the group completed the program, those who did continue working with economic healing began to see some amazing results. What may be most impressive, however, is that the group's exercises have been replicated since that time by countless groups and individuals over many decades, causing many others to attest to the validity of this material. Some of the exercises and disciplines undertaken by various groups and individuals have included the following:

• Daily prayer and meditation, not only to facilitate personal attunement and getting in touch with one's spiritual core but also to assist in overcoming any fear of lack.

• Ongoing work with personal relationships—at home, school, work—wherever they may be. Rather than seeing people as personal challenges that have to be put up with, the Cayce readings encourage us instead to approach all of our relationships with the ideal of "What am I supposed to be learning from this person?" or "What is this person trying to teach me about myself?"

- Being a good steward of the resources that have been entrusted to you. This includes paying bills promptly, not overspending or over-indulging, giving yourself the freedom to buy what you *need* (although not necessarily everything you *want*), and tithing of both money and time without thought of receiving something in return.
- Finally, it is also a good idea to keep an ongoing chart of your progress. This chart can include your daily prayer and meditation time, the success of paying off your debts, the notation of any surprise economic assistance that has come your way, personal tithing, positive experiences with improving your relationships, and so forth.

By working with these ideas, many individuals and groups have found the Edgar Cayce information extremely helpful. This book of verbatim excerpts from the Cayce readings has been compiled to provide an understanding of economic healing and personal prosperity, and suggestions for improving personal financials by working with universal laws and spiritual principles. The approach found in the Edgar Cayce readings for achieving personal material success is about much more than money. It is an approach that encourages individuals to use what they have in hand and to discover and live out their life's mission. It is an approach that admonishes people to become good stewards of the resources they have been entrusted with and ultimately to be able to use every experience encountered in life to become all that they were meant to be.

Kevin J. Todeschi
Executive Director & CEO
Edgar Cayce's A.R.E. / Atlantic University

1

●

Selected Individual Case Histories

Reading 333–1
49–Year–Old Male, Sales Engineer

Gertrude Cayce: You will have before you the body and enquiring mind of [333], who is at ... N.Y., who seeks consideration, advice and guidance, from the Master and the Creative Forces, in regard to the worldwide economic problem which confronts himself and family, together with the great masses of common people struggling for they know not what. You will answer the questions which he has sincerely, respectfully and faithfully submitted.

Edgar Cayce: We have the body, the enquiring mind, [333]; also those conditions, economic and otherwise, that confront the body.

In this relation, there are ever those elements, as was given of old, confronting each and every individual: "There is today set before thee good and evil, life and death. Choose thou whom ye will serve," and let the answer ever be, "Others may do as they may, but for me and my house, we will serve the *living* God." Not one that may not listen or harken to the cry of those that are faithful. One that is not unmindful of the fear, the doubt, that stalks abroad in the land at this particular period in the history of the land when greed, avarice, misunderstanding, has taken the judgement away from many and they struggle for that they know not what. Will all come and—even those that fear—but open their minds, their hearts, their souls, to that cry that has ever been to His peoples, "Will ye be my people, I will be your God"—"Are not two sparrows sold for a farthing? Consider the lilies of the field, how they toil not, neither do they spin, or the grass—that today is and tomorrow is cast in the oven." Whether ye live or whether ye die, ye are in the Lord, and let Him have His way with thee, for He does not suffer even the unfaithful to be tempted without preparing a way of escape. If the righteous shall scarcely be saved, where does the ungodly appear?

Then, use those talents thou hast in hand day by day, and there is given that thou hast need of, will ye but turn your heart, your mind, your soul, to seeking how in loving kindness ye may show in some measure that love, that faith, that confidence, that is aroused in thine own breast with the knowledge that He is in *thine* holy temple; for thine body is indeed the temple of the living God, and let the desires then of the eye, the weaknesses of the flesh, the call for those things that so easily beset thyself, keep silent—*wait* ye on the Lord. Not in some great manifestation that would make for tempestuous doubts in the lives of many, but here a little, there a little, ye that are the salt of the earth, *preserve* same in thine *own* heart, that the *Lord* may have *His* way; for He has not willed that *any* should perish, but that *all* may present their bodies a *living* sacrifice, holy, acceptable unto Him, for it is but a reasonable service.

That the cares of this world, the deceitfulness of place, position, that is sought oft among men, in the owning of houses, lands, and of those things that would wean men's hearts away from following in the straight and narrow path—but know *He* knows what ye have need of before ye ask Him, and wilt thou keep thine heart He will even open the heavens to pour out a blessing upon thee.

In *this* manner, then, should self meet those conditions that seem to confront self at this time. Not that one takes not thought, but by taking thought let it be rather, "Are the courts of my temple a dwelling place of the living God? Or have I rather set up those idols of the earth that are earthy?" And as self *finds* the way clarified by the keeping of the courts and the temple cleansed, "Make not my Father's house a den—"Rather let thy yeas be yea and thy nays be nay, that *He* may come in the heat of the day or the cool of the evening and converse with thee in the courts of thine own temple; for thus doth He speak among men, and thus doth men find that which overcomes fear; for when fear enters, then doth one allow the doors of the temple to be broken up, and there enters in thoughts of the carnal forces that ever war with man, with man's good intent. These kept clean bring the glory of the Father through the Way that the Son has opened for all who seek His face. "The cattle are mine, as the silver and the gold, saith the Lord. These have been prepared that mine children shall not want, even in a *weary* land," but as the rock that casts shadows for those that are athirst, and brings forth its waters that those may be supplied who seek in the shadow of same, so in *this* temple of thine know He will guide, guard and direct in the way that *thou* may become a rock for thine brother; for he that lendeth to the Lord has covered much that may be called amiss by others. *Keep* the way clear.

Ready for questions.

(Q) *Am I wrong in giving thought to the morrow, when I should be placing confidence in divine influence, or trust in God?*

(A) Use rather the opportunities day by day in such a manner that the *glory* of the Lord may be shown in the strength of the mind, of the body, to meet the emergencies that arise as concerning the secular things of life; for as these offices may appear to become more slack in this or that direction, the greater *faith*—rather than confidence—in His promises makes for *strength* in body and mind to meet those things necessary. Let the *desires* of the Physical grow less, as the desires of the spiritual would make thee strong in His might.

(Q) *Am I among those who shall be blessed by being found so doing when the Lord cometh?*

(A) Keep thy face to the light, and the shadows of doubt fall *far* behind. So thou wilt find thy name written among those who loved his fellowman, even as He walked among men—called them His brother—gave of that bounty supplied by the closer communion day by day. "Give us *this* day our *daily* bread. *Forgive*, O Lord, as I forgive my brother." In walking in this light does the strength to do the physical deeds come in the body, even as the strength to bear His own cross, even as the strength to give, "Father, *forgive* them—they know not what they do!" This brought ministering from the Father of light, the Father of power, the Father of love to man, that we are *his* brothers and heirs to the

Kingdom of light through ministering in word, in deed, to our fellowman in His Name; for there be no name named under heaven that brings hope, joy, life, as the *Name* of the *Christ* among men!

(Q) Am I wrong in remaining in my present employment? [Sales Engineer for steel and metal products company]

(A) Remain in the employment, that there may come—*with* the building up on every side—that which will enable self, and those the body serves, to *know* even the rocks and hills cry out, "*blessed* is he who comes in the name of the Lord!"

Does the remuneration in the present surroundings not supply that necessary to meet those payments that may come upon the earthly abode, then those surroundings—as well as the abilities to obtain through other channels those means that will enable you to supply that lacking—will be given thee in no uncertain measures, *will* there be held, "I *am* the Lord's—He *is* my defense—in Him *will* I put my trust—and I *will* be faithful to my brother to the best of my physical and my mental abilities." Not becoming a pest in speaking of those things. "When there is the cry for bread, doth He give them a stone?" Rather give him a portion of that *thou* hast, and together *seek* the Lord!

(Q) Are the men who are paying me a wage doing so in full measure of their ability, justice and consideration for my responsibilities?

(A) As ye measure, so shall it be measured to you again! "The Lord *bless* them, the Lord keep them, and make His face to shine upon them, in such measures that *together in* the trials may there come the blessed understanding that all must work together to meet the measures that are being brought to all during this seeking period of those that have wandered far afield," for the Lord *keepeth* those that fear—yea, love and trust in the fear of the Lord!

These are capable of being approached by responsibilities and measures builded upon self. "In the way ye would have them deal with you, deal ye with them!"

(Q) Would it be right for me to seek employment during the night hours with a wholesale bakery or gas service station, to help increase my income?

(A) Seek and ye shall find! Keep in the way of the Lord and the way is opened unto thee to meet those needs for thine self and for thine dependent ones, as well as that that may be given or lent to the Lord through aiding thy brother! *Seek*—when needed.

We are through for the present.

Reading 78–4
23–Year–Old Male

Gertrude Cayce: You will have before you the body and the enquiring mind of [78], present in this room. This entity seeks advice and guidance concerning the difficulties of his present position. Considering the
general conditions throughout the country as they affect this individual,
you will give such suggestions and council that will aid this body at this
time. You will also answer the questions which I will ask you regarding
this individual.

Edgar Cayce: We have the body, the enquiring mind, [78]—this we
have had before. In considering the conditions and circumstances that
confront, and that influence the body at the present, many and varied
may be the manners in which the entity may view same. Not only as
how circumstances, conditions and surroundings affect the mental attitude of the body, but how the body is affected by same, as well as the
outlook upon life the body gathers from the study of, contemplation of,
self's position in its various phases, and *how* same *is* affected by self's
attitude *and* outlook towards conditions.

In advising one as concerning the manner of activity, or action toward conditions under such circumstance, much might be said as to *just*
advice—as to do or *don't* do this or that. The *conditions* as to be *met* are—
What *is* the view or attitude to be assumed or taken as respecting *definite*
conditions as exist in the life, as to outlook mentally, outlook physically,
relationships to others, others' relationships to self. These should be the
first considerations. Not only as duties, not only as privileges, but also
as opportunities.

Do not get *this* position, however, as to ever be condemning self *or*
another for that as exists in one's own life. If this be of self's own making, then know better than to do the same thing again. If felt of another's
making, then *use* same rather as a stepping stone for *better* understanding and application of self.

As to the conditions and the movements to be made: Many are the
opportunities; only one would say "Just one do I want", as would the

entity. Then, ready for questions.

(Q) *Just where and in what place may this body find employment suited to his capabilities? and how should he go about to secure same?*

(A) Under the present circumstances, present conditions as exist in and throughout the country—not as to *seeking* an opportunity; rather go about to *make* one. That there have been promises that have become questionable and that are doubted at times by self and by others, these will materialize—but not as *soon* as may be desired, but be not *faint* hearted over *any* circumstance; rather *use* the present conditions, the present surroundings, and make for self for the time being that as will enable, will better fit the body for what is, or what may, or what will come.

(Q) *Will the job promised in connection with the Chase National Bank in New York through David McKenzie develop within two months?*

(A) Rather in *three* months there will be an opportunity. There are others, and other channels—as we find—that would offer better opportunities.

(Q) *What channel will offer the best opportunities?*

(A) Those as surround the body in the present, as we would find, would offer better and more of that in keeping with the eventualities, or the working *towards* those as would be better suited for the body . . .

(Q) *When will be the correct time for me to carry out my contemplated marriage?*

(A) When self has succeeded in gaining hold of self in a manner to know that the future for self and the obligation taken is, at least, in a *satisfactory* manner assured for the present.

(Q) *Please give me any advice regarding the maintaining a more perfect mental and physical balance.*

(A) In that as outlined may be that as an alignment of thought in a manner and direction as will give the proper attitude for the body, and the entity, in its activity. *Not* as a *servile* attitude; *not* as one in a position of embarrassment; neither as one that would laud or applaud self for anything accomplished *within* self—either physically *or* mentally; but rather in *humbleness* of heart, mind *and* body *to* be a channel for an ideal of *whatever* making self may choose; were it only to *that* ideal of self's relationship to an individual, to self, or to the creative forces—for they are *one*, and each are a pattern of the other.

(Q) Should I see Mr. McKenzie on Jan. 15th concerning position?

(A) That would be dependent upon what arrangements, or what are the determined factors in other conditions that have been suggested.

Then, let those work out—for these are as the conditions or positions as they would present themselves:

In a position of association in the banking interest, represents or presents this:

A place; not a position, but one that bespeaks of an association that lends to an individual that of an honorable, venerable, and a position that is *well*-spoken of—but supplying *little* of this world's goods, other than *through* some *questionable* channels—which, *to* the body, the mind, the consciousness of the entity, must sooner or later become abhorrent, unless a soon success is gained.

In the channels of a minor position of a servant, in an aptitude or position of an attendant keeper of a place of not wholly amusement, but of gratifying some of the needs, desires, and pleasures of others, makes for a lowly *beginning*—from the same standard of views, but a growth wherein there would be the development of an *ideal* that may be builded upon with a *sure* basis.

Reading 78–5
25–Year–Old Male, Follow–Up Reading

Gertrude Cayce: You will have before you the body and enquiring mind of [78], ..., Alabama, and his connections and associations especially as related to his securing employment as quickly as possible and his contemplated marriage. You will advise him as to the correct course to pursue and answer the questions which he has submitted.

Edgar Cayce: Yes, we have the body, the enquiring mind, [78], this we have had before; also those conditions, those circumstances that confront the body in the present.

Now, as we find, recently there have been some circumstances and conditions that tend to alter the whole general trend of relations.

And while there will be required some time for adjustments for the body, if there are the serious considerations in the present of the contemplated relations as to marriage, that which has been proposed in the manner of the relations and associations as respecting all parties con-

cerned would be the better channel for the body to make the definite
decisions in following that line of endeavor.

If there are those doubts within self as to whether this body would
be able to cope with, or to meet those conditions which so alter the
outlook upon the whole activities of the body-physical, then it would
be well that there be the separations entirely from such contempla-
tions; and that the endeavors be rather in those lines in which he has
associated, in the first city to which the body went seeking the employment. And through those channels in which the body expended its
efforts may there be found that employment, as soon as there is sufficient time for the adjustment of general conditions—or by the first of
June. This would allow sufficient lapse for the adjusting of conditions in
the immediate surroundings, and time for the contemplation of those
conditions as related to those suggestions that have been made.

Ready for questions . . .

(Q) *Please give such advice and counsel as will aid me in getting a better hold on
myself and in meeting the various conditions that arise from time to time.*

(A) A self-analysis of the desires and wishes, and the *fixing* of self as
toward some ideal outside of self will enable the body to better meet—
mentally and materially—those conditions and problems that present
themselves from time to time.

These, as the body—the mental abilities—will recognize, are necessary; for one to *have* an ideal to make for the impulse and activities
towards working for some conditions as outside of self.

(Q) *Any other advice for this body at this time?*

(A) Hold to that which has been grounded in the latent impulses (as
we have given), for the abilities are there. The faults are in that the
ideals are shattered.

We are through for the present.

Reading 78–7
25-Year-Old Male, Follow-Up Reading

Ready for questions.

(Q) *When and to whom shall I go to find employment at this time?*

(A) First, we would consider all the conditions that surround the body
from the economic angle; from the associations and relations that have

existed, that do exist, in the present; also that which we have given through these channels as to what line of endeavor would offer for the body the environ that would bring about the better or more apt conditions, that would be in keeping with the abilities, the intents, the purposes that are innate and manifested in the experience of the entity.

Then, considering all these conditions, the environs, the surroundings, the conditions, and the experiences that the body has had to the present, we would advise that the present environs and the surroundings in the home associations be considered.

In the present it may appear that these would not justify the body continuing, nor justify the desires and the conditions for the body's outlook or the training of the body in its mental attributes (considering the associations in those activities of the body, and the body's parents' association). Yet, these have been—and these are, in the main—those sources from which the present supply of the material necessities must arise.

Hence it would be well that the body accomplish what it may in the present environs; and, during the period, take the necessary training—through a correspondence course—*for* the position that we have given should be, or would be, a satisfactory environ, that would be the beginning of the associations that would bring about satisfactory relationships.

Then, by the beginning of the next season either in the early portion of the year or, at least, by the spring or summer seasons, there should be the opening through these same channels, for the study and the preparations for a satisfactory connection and association for the body.

And, in the present conditions, those surroundings, those conditions that have been brought about by the activities of the body, the better connections would be in the associations at the present time; and these would offer for the body the better preparations for that which may be brought to pass in the experience of the body.

(Q) *Is it advisable at this time, or any time in the future, for [W...] and I to get married?*

(A) We would advise it at once, if satisfactory with those conditions that may be brought about for all concerned in the present—and would make for the best in the new environs that will develop. Be patient. Be persistent.

Because it is apparent, in the mind of the body, that the body may be looked upon as having failed in accomplishing or in conquering those associations and connections, should inspire rather than make discouragements in the body's experience.

Those individuals that are worth the name of being manly, or godly manly, are those that use the discouraging moments rather as the testing periods and make of them stepping-stones for that which may be accomplished in earnestness.

And remember, that which is to be constructive in the mental, the material or the spiritual life, must have its inception, its basis for its activities, in that which is true, pure, honest, sincere. Or, the body-mind, the mental forces, should feed more and more upon those things that are the *builders* . . .

(Q) *Is there any special school of correspondence recommended?*

(A) There are several different ones. The Cincinnati school, as we find, would be the most profitable—for the training as a whole. Or, the Buffalo school. Either are well, and both give—or prompt—the association and connections with the United Hotel Associations, that may present—for the interest and for the activities of the body—that which would be in line with those suggestions we have given.

These may be found advertised in many different groups. The LaSalle course is very good, from Chicago. But, as we find, the Cincinnati or Buffalo school connections are the most satisfactory for the hotel training.

(Q) *Give me any advice or counsel that might help me find a job and financial independence.*

(A) We would advise beginning where we are; using that in hand, making considerations for those about self, those dependent upon self; taking on those responsibilities that will not only aid but add to the respectability, the affability, the conditions that make for building character.

And, most of all, do not lose faith in self nor self's abilities, when trusting in the divine influences that are the birthright of every soul.

Reports of Reading 2071–2
33–Year–Old Female
Letter excerpt from [2071]

... felt that I should have an immediate business reading. I seem to have been surrounded with a great deal of confusion and uncertainty lately. Directional suggestions would be very welcome. I feel that I have made up for any transgressions in past experiences, for my way has been very difficult and I have by no means had the success some other artists enjoy—and certainly no "lucky breaks". There are several fields of endeavor in which I am seeking to earn a livelihood—even ... [my friends] do not know how serious my financial problem is, for one does not always like one's friends to know.

To be perfectly honest with you—I am a little tired of it all (that is, the constant striving for maintenance) and, while I do not say this in a spirit of fault-finding nor dissatisfaction, I would be thoroughly content to let someone else carry the burden for a while . . . To put it frankly, neither of my husbands has supported me or contributed to my support (and, as a matter of fact, their own). I alone am to blame for letting it continue but I hesitate to tear my life apart to make changes . . .

I am enclosing a set of questions which include my main interests at the moment—also a check for five dollars, which is all I can spare at the moment.

Letter excerpt from [2071]'s secretary, offering additional information

My dear Mr. Cayce:

Miss [2071] has given you what I believe to be a very frank and complete description of her present situation. However, I would like to add a few words to what she has already told you—believing it will help both you and her by so doing.

Naturally, she would be restricted in telling you some of the more flattering phases of her existence—and also she has neglected to ask you the questions which seems to torment her and come to her mind most frequently—that is, what *is* it that is wrong with her life—what is the thing that is holding her back, and why is it that she remains in the sidelines now while others, with far less talent and capabilities, either in a musical, cultural, educational, business or entertainment standpoint, are riding the ladder of success and enjoying the fruits of what she has helped to establish and create. Even her ideas are taken from her before she has a chance to formulate them actually—she has "pioneered" many a song—an idea—a show—later to hear someone else make a hit out of material stolen from her. Will you *please* be kind enough (confidentially, if you wish) to tell me what is holding back—what this weight is that is holding her feet on the ground when she is meant to soar?

All of those who know her, hold her in high esteem and respect—she is much loved and admired not only for her talents, but her graciousness and charm—and her good heart, her helping hand, and her genuine sincerity and interest in the good of others. She is so much more highly evolved than the average run of person—it seems incredible that after years of hard work and intelligent appliance, she should not enjoy greater achievement. She is so tired—so discouraged sometimes. And yet, she always has a smile and an encouraging word to other in distress and seems to lead them upward. And yet her own life falls miserably apart—why?

I have been with Miss [2071] for five years and know her better than anyone else in the world—and, I dare say, love her more. I know her to be an angel—too good, I guess, to be smart. She is a creator of beauty in its every expression—in music, in song, in grace—in the decoration of her home—in dress—she is born to create. I am telling you these things so that you might have a more intimate glimpse of her.

Reading 2071–3
45–Year–Old Female, Singer and Composer

Gertrude Cayce: You will have before you the body and enquiring mind of [2071], at home in ..., Conn., who seeks information, advice and guidance as to her work, her domestic and material affairs. You will answer the questions, as I ask them:

Edgar Cayce: Yes, we have the body, the enquiring mind, [2071]; this we have had before.

Many changes have come in the relationships and the activities of the entity since last we had these conditions here. Some have been, for a time, most pleasing—in a material sense. Some have become very disappointing. Others have brought fear and confusion in the experience of this entity.

As we find, it might be well given, "I told you so"—if the entity would analyze conditions, not merely from the material angle or the material success, or the material disappointments, but from the intent and purpose which has been *at time* the promptings of the entity in its dealings with and in its relationships to others.

This should be taken into consideration with that advice, that counsel which has been and was indicated in those suggestions through this channel—when there was the analyzing of promptings in the experience of the entity from its sojourns through this material plane.

From the experiences it is evidenced that the entity finds self in the present with abilities that have not, to the entity's manner of analysis, produced the material results in the present experience. Yet those abilities to bring harmony and peace in the experiences of others, through the use of faculties in voice, in harmony, in such activities, are evidenced.

Is the fault, then, in the manner in which these abilities have been presented to those who are longing for such harmony in their own life? Or is it the fault of the entity's attempting to present that which is nonexistent in its own experience?

Remember, God is not mocked. This is an unfailing, an indisputable law—a fact. For if the promptings are from the heart, the mind, the soul—not that self may be exalted, not that self may be in the limelight in fame or in fortune, but wholly, unreservedly trusting in Him and acting in that way and manner towards thy fellow man—His promises are sure, that ye *shall* succeed in whatsoever ye undertake!

This success, then, is not as the world looks on success—such as bringing others to thy feet, that they may do thee honor. Rather it is such that he that is the servant of all is the greatest among his fellow men.

The fault here, as we find, lies greatly—then—in the direction to which the abilities have been put.

Those who have been in the position to make contact with the various offices through which the services might be rendered, or through which the abilities might be expressed, or through which the love of its fellow men might be made manifest—whether in the radio work or the skits, or the acting in parts, or in any activity in which there might be brought notice—these have been rather working with the key purpose for material gain.

Hence *we* would give, first: Consider well thy contact agent, or the one in whom ye have put confidence as to the channels for expressing thy abilities, or the one who is thy agent for such activities.

For the world, the public, the individual, still seeks, longs for, desires earnestly, that ye are capable of giving, and have the ability to give to others through such channels.

Ready for questions.

(Q) What would be the most important move to make at this time?

(A) Get a good agent! and one that considers the abilities *for* the love of expressing same, as well as for material gains! for these—the gains—should be the *result of* such love shown in thy activity!

(Q) Is there one you would suggest, or through whom my work should be presented?

(A) Hunt—hunt—hunt—*hunt* 'em!

These will *not* be laid down as definite individuals from here! Do you gain a voice by wishing for one? Do you gain association and love by wishing for it, or by showing same in thine own experience?

Those who would have success *mustn't* flit it away upon those who care only for the moment!

(Q) Should I remain in professional work? If so, what branch?

(A) The radio is the better—those skits that combine both the voice and the partial acting.

(Q) How can I further the publication of my songs?

(A) Make them popular in the minds of individuals by the manner in which ye are capable of expressing them, in voice, through the mediums for reaching the people.

(Q) How can I make contacts to meet the right people?

(A) Through the proper kind of contact person.

(Q) Did I do right by moving out to my place in Connecticut?

(A) As we find, if those activities are set in motion that have first been given through this channel—as to that to be met in self, and then the proper presentation of the abilities, though they are long before the public—yes. But these should or must be kept burning, even as the home fires where harmony and peace may abide. One may not rest upon what *has* been, but must be ready to show—each and every day, in each and every contact—that self is one willing to give an answer for the faith that is within.

Thus there may be brought friends, love, success, happiness, *joy*—as a *result of* something given by self!

(*Q*) *Under present circumstances, what should I do about my house?*

(A) Prepare those ways and means to take care of same.

(*Q*) *How can I reduce my blood pressure?*

(A) This also has been indicated in the information previously given through this channel, and if adhered to will keep same in a normal manner.

We are through for the present.

(*Q*) *(Left out of original copy) Will my present husband ever amount to anything, or do you see a change for the better in the future?*

(A) This depends upon who is to judge.

These as we find are some of thy disappointments.

If there will be the setting of self's house in order, in relationships to that which is the motivative purpose and influence within self, there will be brought harmonious relationships—*if* not here, in others.

Reading 3976–14
"World Affairs" Reading on the Depression and the Economy

Hugh Lynn Cayce: You will give at this time that which will aid each individual present in understanding the reason and comprehensibility of that through which we as individuals are passing and experiencing in the situation economically at this time.

Edgar Cayce: Yes, we have conditions economically as they exist in this land at the present time. In giving, then, an analysis of such in a manner that may be helpful for those that would seek to know themselves and the causes for the present general conditions:

To be sure, these have been approached from many varied angles by those who have sought, are seeking, to find the answers to such conditions in their own experiences; and by many that are seeking, and have sought, that there might be aid, understanding, comprehension, in the experience of others.

In the very nature, though, of a nation, a people, there are some fundamental principles upon which the economic and the soul life of a nation must be founded, if such a people, such a nation, is to remain true to that which is the birthright of every soul; to pursue that which will give it as an individual the right to manifest that it would worship in its Creator.

For, the first law that has been given to man from the beginning is: "Thou shalt have no other gods before me." And when man has faltered, has altered that, which has deprived others from giving expression to that birthright, that command that has come to man throughout the ages, then there arises that which creates those things that are the fruits of the evil influences that are in the earth. Such as: Hate, jealousy, avarice, and the like. These make for the creating of those conditions in all walks of life for power, for position, for the love of money and that it will bring in its associations in the lives of individuals. And, as there has been just this experience in the affairs of the nation as a nation, the nation as a nation is passing through that period when each soul must turn to that thought within of what is its relation to the Creative Forces in its experience; and each soul must ask itself what it as a soul is going to do about that command that was given, and that is the privilege of every soul; to show forth that very law of love that is the birthright of every soul. For, with that command has come ever that to which mankind may expect to find himself reduced when he has forgotten that which is his *first* duty, and the second which is likened unto it; "Thou shalt love thy neighbor as thyself."

Then, this condition has been the experience in the greater portion of the whole nation, the whole world. For, that is the experience of the individual that makes for the creating in his environ, his surrounding, of that which breeds strife, that which breeds hate, that which breeds malice, that which breeds selfishness.

The next law, as man knows, is that "Like begets like." And His injunction has been: "The worlds may pass away, but my Word shall not pass away; and ye shall pay to every farthing—and, as ye do unto your neighbor, as ye purpose in your heart, so will it be measured unto you." And when conditions arise that make for distress, whether they be in body, in mind, in the economic influences in the experience of any, *sin* lieth at *thy* door. Not thine neighbor's! Blame not the other fellow. Seek first to know within self that which has prompted thee, and when thou hast set thine house in order, when thou hast made thine peace with thine own conscience (that would smite thee, if ye will look within your own heart), then may ye find the answers that will come to every soul that seeks. For, as He has given to those of old, He is the same yesterday, today and forever. Think not as to who will ascend into heaven to bring down comfort and ease to thine own aching heart, or who will go over the seas to bring that which may be of a recompense within thine own experience, but lo! ye shall find it in your own heart!

Thus has the lawgiver given, and thus has He said who has set the way to make the intercession for man: "I will not leave thee comfortless, if ye will seek to do my biddings."

Many would say, "Yea, this is beautiful; yet it does not feed the hungry nor clothe those that are naked, nor make shelter for those that are cold."

Who is—Who *is*—the representative of the Father in the earth? Hath not He committed unto mankind the keeping of his brother? Hast thou answered that question that has been of old in thine experience; "Am I My Brother's Keeper?" The answer that should ring in the heart and soul of every individual is: "Know ye not that the blood of your brother crieth unto me from the ground!"

So, in the experience of those that have sent and made the conditions are greed, selfishness; that has been practiced in the minds, in the lives, in the experience of the nation. Think not any soul, "Yea, that is true for the other fellow." But it applies to Jim, to Tom, to those in ordinary walks of life, to those who have been given those powers in high places, those that have wealth about them; *they* are the oppressors; yea, look within thine own heart! Hast thou not practiced the same? For, as it has been given, "Yea, though there be only ten just men, they may save the city; they may save the nation; they may save the world," if they will but *practice* in their daily experience that which has been the command from the first: "Thou shalt love the Lord thy God with all thine heart, and thy neighbor as thyself."

This is the basis of all *spiritual* law; and to you would there be given as this:

There is no activity in the experience of man that has not its inception or purpose in the spirit of those injunctions but what *must* fail; unless it is founded in the spirit of truth.

Hence each would ask, then: "What must I do about it; not what shall this, that or the other ruler, other office holder, or the other individual do" but each should ask, "What must I do about the economic conditions in which we find ourselves?"

So live each day, each hour, as to put into practice those precepts, those influences in thine own life, and in the life of all ye contact day by day. For, He hath said, "Though ye wander far afield, if ye will cry unto me, if ye will ask, if ye will draw unto me, I will draw nigh unto thee; and my help, my arm is not short as man's counting of shortness, but will bring to thee speedily that which is the desire of thine heart, if it is conceived in righteousness."

Reading 3976–24
"World Affairs" Reading

(Q) *As has been indicated through these channels, money is the root cause of the general economic unbalance of our country. Will you give specifically the reasons for this statement and the approach that can be made toward correction of the money order as operated today.*

(A) Fear on the part of those who control or direct the investing of capital into channels that give the greater outlet of their characters of outlet.

As to how this may be corrected—it is only through patience, persistence, and a *return* to the trust in God, and *not* in the power or the might of self.

Reading 683–1
43–Year–Old Female, Chiropractor. Main problem was cited as being financial

Edgar Cayce: Yes, we have the entity and those relations with the universe and universal forces, that are latent and manifested in the personalities of the entity now known as, or called, [683].

In entering the present experience we find, from sojourns in the earth and the application of the abilities of the entity in such sojourns, not only those influences of the astrological that are in the mental application but those of the more material in the numerological, as well as in tones and colors, have influenced and do influence the entity. Not always in this experience has there been the proper interpretation of such influences. And they in their application by the entity have at times been rather confusing; thus causing some disturbance in the relationships of the entity with other minds as related to the body-mind of the entity. Hence in giving that which may be helpful, hopeful and developing for the entity, we will give that which we find here from those records that have been made by the entity in the earth's plane in its own soul or spiritual development. Then analyzing these they may become as useful experiences in the entity's application of them in the present experience.

Do not confuse, then, mental experiences that are innate and those that come through spiritual awareness or awakening within self with those that are of an earthly urge by having—in the mental body, with the environs of a physical surrounding—experienced urges that may confuse; yet know all have their place in the experience of an entity, an individual, in the application of its abilities. Learn and practice, then, the first things first; as this: The entity, the soul, is supreme in itself as related to any circumstance or influence, whether an environmental, hereditary or a passing condition, through the *will*—that is the gift of the Creator. And *if* the entity in its seeking applies that which is shown within self it may *never* confuse self as to the correct, positive, direct manner in which to apply the impulse that motivates an activity towards the application of that gained within self. For it is not in knowledge alone but rather in the application of such understanding that the mental body, the soul body, grows. Hence, as has been given to all: Study to show thyself—*thyself*—approved unto thy Maker, divining the words of truth.

So, in the application of that *thou knowest* does there come the knowledge, the understanding of what, of where, of how, the next step, the next activity, is to be taken . . .

From Venus we find the creating, or making, or imposing into the entity throughout its experience the innate seeking—seeking—for that which in the material plane is an expression of, and manifestation of, that which Venus indicates in the thoughts of man; as it does in its environs; Love, helpfulness, hopefulness, optimism in its broader, greater sense. Yet these experiences in the entity's application have been so often shattered. And as we shall see, we will find out the *why* through the experiences in the earth, and how this has been builded in the experience as a karmic condition (as termed by some); for these are words—just words, but carry—as does an impulse from within—a meaning to an individual entity that to the entity is *all* its own. Hence, as given, it *is* the expression that makes for growth within the soul forces of an entity. Hence it may be said of the entity in this direction, *growth* has been and *is* the experience of the entity in this sojourn. Then, the lesson to be learned by the entity in this direction in this experience is *patience*. This has, through the very expression of love to the fellow man by the entity, been a drawback. For oft has the entity in the experience, in losing patience with others, with self, turned to material urges that have brought confusion. Hence the warnings: Judge spiritual urges in spiritual realms by spiritual things, and material and mental urges only by material application.

Yet this growth in the activities in the present from the Venus sojourn has not always been tempered with a Mercurian influence, for it has been rather in an adverse position—through an influence of Saturn's activity in the experience. Hence we find that tendency for the change when there were those disturbing factors in the experience of the entity in the present, to turn to seek in another direction. This is from an influence, an indwelling in Saturn where even the influences may have been perfected; yet they come as tests, as trials, as experiences, that the injunction which has been given may be fulfilled in the experience of the soul; "Stand ye steadfast *today* and see the glory of thy God *within!*"

Hence these have been as tendencies for the entity in the experience to fail here, in that it turned occasionally to those things that bespoke rather of the material things, or the influences from without appeared to be as necessities for the moment; losing patience with this, that, the other. Patience is not as a passive thing, but patience is necessary in the experience of each soul rather as a *positive*, *active* thing *within* the application of same. Thus an entity becomes aware of its own soul and that soul's vision of the glories that may be its experience in its associations with those promises in the creative force of the soul along that *is* eternal and in the image of the Maker.

The Jupiterian influences, we find, have made and do make for—in the expressions of the entity—a wide, broad field of activity; which to an unstable one in the position of that indicated as the experience of the entity, while it has its advantageous experience also may become the very influence of a stumbling experience for a soul. But the vision here is, as we find, as it grows—the entity's ability in the application of those attributes that have made for the expending of self in love, in hope, and though wandering afield at times in its inner self—those attributes of patience become as applicable things in the experience with that already gained. Then do those benevolent influences from those visions and experiences in Jupiter bring a field of activity for the entity that will make for happiness, contentment, harmony, and those things that are of the earth-earthy, yet may be used in the material expressions of those benevolent influences that have been the privilege of the entity in its application to have gained in Venus. Hence we will find, if the entity will hold fast to that which is good, rightly divining the words of truth, the days must come in the earth yet when many will call it blessed and count it a priviledge to have known, to have been priviledged to have been a helpmeet for the entity in its activities in the earth . . .

"If ye will keep my commandments in thine activities to thy fellow man, I will bring to thy remembrance those things necessary for the assurance that I will abide with thee." Ponder these well in thine inner self, for they may become those things whereupon thou may depend, where thou may gain strength, where thou may find that succor, that aid, that will bear thee up lest *thou*—in thine lack of understanding—dash thine head against a stone. For His love would constrain thee, even as *thou* in thine expression would constrain to show that love thou has gained in thine experience, even as this—the love for the souls of men that are the expression in material bodies, flesh, of the love of the Father . . .

Again in the expression in the present the entity has found many of these confusing at times, for when there has been the application to the material things in the present many have called the entity impractical. And the lack of the patience that was attained in that experience makes for periods when doubts and confusions arise in the experience of the entity in the present. Yet, as has been indicated, if the entity will turn within it may gain the lessons again that were given by that Teacher among men, learn again those messages with which it strengthened those when the fear of death was upon those that were young and strong in body, those that were old and were being separated from those they loved the most in the earth, and how that strengthening cry went up; "Lo, I am with thee always, even unto the end of the world! Put thine trust in me and thou wilt know that thy Redeemer liveth, and thou shalt see Him as He is." For He has promised that He will comfort and strengthen and sustain those that to their fellow man show forth the love of the Father. And he that doeth those kindnesses to his fellow man lendeth to the Lord, and He has prepared those mansions—even as He has given, "I prepare a place where I am there ye may be also." If the entity will ponder upon these messages that the entity gave in those experiences as Sylvia, the shepherdess, the one that strengthened so many in those days, there will come a strength, a glory, a vision, an understanding that will raise thee up above. But "He that is the servant of all is the greatest among thee!"

. . . As to the abilities of the entity in the present, then, and that to which it may attain and how:

As has been indicated by the experiences of the entity in that which is innate and builded within the self, study to show thyself approved unto Him. For if the heart is singing with the beauties and joys that may come in the service to the fellow man, it bespeaks of those things that answer from within as to the life being made as a channel of blessing to the fellow man—and *in* the path of glory for the companionship with Him.

Ready for questions.

(Q) What shall I do to be financially successful at this time?

(A) First find in self that in which the applications of the abilities thou hast in body and in mind are founded, and seek thou those realms wherein these may be put into practical application, and in the associations of those relations whereunto thou may bring to others not only tenets but living truths within self; and these will bring the returns as their natural consequence. For, as He has given, man may labor in this or that field; God alone can give, does give, the increase.

Let thy life and thy activities with thy fellow man be in accord with that thou hast determined, and leave the increase of the financial or material gains in his hands.

(Q) *Are there any special persons that could help me?*

(A) They will be pointed out to thee; for, as He has given, "I will guide, I will direct thee, in the way that thou shouldst go."

(Q) *Am I breaking any special law that causes conditions to be as they are?*

(A) As indicated, study that thou hast given; for ye shall find. He that seeks shall find. Study to show thyself approved unto thy Maker, correctly *divining*, dividing, the words of truth.

Reading 683-2
43-Year-Old Female, Chiropractor, Follow-Up Reading

In the material associations, in the material connections, then, do with thy might what thy hand finds to do *today*. For sufficient unto the day is the good as well as the evil thereof. For as He hath given in thee that thou may be the channel, the representative, the agent—yea, the very representative in flesh of Him, then act in thine inner self, act in thine outward expression, as though thou wert (for thou art!) His child, and are heir to all the glories *here*, *now*, of His kingdom. *Not* in the future, not of the past! For in the eternal *now* is He *active* in thee.

And ye will find, as the days come, as the weeks pass, that ye will be shown from day to day the next step. For He is thy God and thy counsel, and thy help, and upon His arm may ye lean; upon His hand may ye be led in the things, the experiences, the conditions through which ye may pass.

Ready for questions.

(Q) *Should I remain in my present occupation or consider a change?*

(A) In the present remain, until thou be shown the more excellent way. For as each soul, each entity, each individuality prepares itself, He will lift it up (as thee); in the material and in the mental things that are necessary for it (as thou) being the greater channel of expressions for Him.

(Q) *Have I any special talent that should be developed?*

(A) As indicated; as ye are able and as ye are given the body to minister to the needs of the physical bodies of many, ye have the talent also to minister at such times (and oh, what an opportunity!) to the mental needs of those that are soul sick as well as in body and mind. Point ye the way, then, to Him at such times. That is a talent; yea, has He not given into the keeping of all, in every walk of life who may minister to the needs of bodily ills, the opportunity to tell others, to tell those physically ill of the love of the Father, of the abilities in Him, of Him who stands between those influences of good and evil, the crossroads of choice, that every one and every soul each day must cross? And ye may point the way—ye that have been endowed, either physically, mentally or spiritually—for such a service. What a responsibility! And so many in thine own field, in thine own understanding, have shirked their duty, have failed Him and put Him to shame who hath said, "In me is life, in me is health, in me is strength." And ye in thy blindness have pointed the other way. Then, minister as is shown thee by Him.

(Q) Will the healing work bring better financial results than in the past few years?

(A) If ye will but take Him as thy partner, if ye will but take Him as thy right hand brother. For the silver and the gold is His, and He alone may *move* the hearts of those that are sick in body and mind, who are beset with the fear of those things that are of the earth, to open their storehouses or their pocketbooks to thine needs. Use that thou hast in hand. If it be true it will be as of His servant who cast his rod or stock or cane, which became as the serpent to those that were of enchantment or of their own knowledge that might show their strength; yea, but that one which was guided of the Lord swallowed them all up. So, in thy ministry to thy fellow man, if ye will but take Him *with* thee in thine heart, in thine seeking to give that as will bring the awakening, it will swallow up those that have spoken unkindly. And thy gentleness of mien, thine understanding of the ills will be as an incense before Him, so that the bounty of thy hand will be poured out as though the windows of heaven were opened for such.

(Q) Is there any special line of the healing work that I should follow to bring better results?

(A) As indicated, take it—as thou hast gained and as thou seekest in the ministrations of same—with Him as thy *partner*, as thine helper, as thine director; so will the ways be opened. For *all* healing is the awakening of that eternal hope that springs anew within the human breast that it may have another opportunity, that it may give and be itself a channel. And as ye open the way through not only the ministry of thy hands but thy word of mouth in telling of Him and His love, it will make not afraid but give and give and give the opportunity to all! But to him that tramples on same it becomes the stumblingstone.

Reading 2275–1
48-Year-Old Female, Masseuse

Then, in analysing, this, there may be references made to the latent and manifested urges; but, as is the experience of the entity, no urge surpasses the will of the individual. And what an entity does about or with the opportunities expressed or manifested, or that become a part of the experience, becomes and should be kept innate, and in those directions to fulfil not merely a destiny but to be a living example of that it, the entity, professes to believe in and holds as its ideal—spiritually, mentally, physically.

And, as this entity does embrace and has embraced in its religious or spiritual concept, the activity should be in keeping with its deepest tenets—not of self-righteousness nor the laudation of self, but of that which is the all-embracing purpose for which God has manifested His love, His purposes among men.

Then, as to the activities in the present—let those things that bring hope, faith and brotherly love be practical applications in the daily associations with its fellow men.

And putting the whole trust, the whole purpose in those activities, the entity need never fear, need never have a doubt or quaver as to what will be accomplished—physically, mentally or spiritually—in this material plane.

The activities during the sojourns of the entity through the material plane have enabled the entity to become associated in this experience with, and to make a practical application of, ways or means to be of material as well as of mental help to others who are afflicted, or who are lacking in the best in their experience . . .

Ready for questions.

(Q) *How may I make my own profession, as a licensed masseuse, more suitable for me?*

(A) By applying in thy daily applications of its good offices that which is best within thee; and with the desire and purpose not merely to have a job, not merely to have a means of achieving material gains, but to do a work entrusted to thee by a divine power that enables thee to be to each soul to whom ye apply thy work, thy profession, a channel, a means of making manifest His love among thy fellow men.

Applied in such a way and manner it *cannot*, it *will not* fail. And ye will find a greater increase. Not by loud boasting, no. But let thy prayer and thy meditation be, as ye make application to others, *"Lord, lead Thou the way!"*

(Q) *How should I go about to get more medical massages?*

(A) As has been offered, accept those channels through which ye may be closely associated with those who are in direct connection with the medical associations and medical treatments.

(Q) *Which of the two offers should I accept?*

(A) Both of these *can* be had, if there is the desire to *work* self to that extent. Otherwise, choose that as appears to be in keeping with that thou purposest to do within thine own conscience.

(Q) *Why did the dentist offer me his office? What does he think of me?*

(A) What thinkest thou of him? The answer is as the reflection of thy thoughts of him!

(Q) *How am I able to establish a clientele for these offices?*

(A) In the manners and ways as indicted. Let each client, each person ye serve, be that as He gave—"He that would be the greatest among you will be and is the servant of all."

In that attitude, in that manner, that way of expressing self, ye *build* that which is creative and helpful; and not only does it bring peace and harmony but love with same—which is so lacking in thy experience!

(Q) *Or is there anything else I can do to make a decent living, and be happy and successful in my occupation?*

(A) In the manner outlined is the better way and manner, as we find indicated from the experience and the application of self through the sojourns as well as the purposes in the present.

(Q) *Should I take a partner?*

(A) In *any* way or manner! Keep too much from partnerships of any nature. Be rather the director thyself; though ye may choose helpers if so desired; but in such be to each one as ye would have that one be to thee—in God's ways and not just for material gains.

Reading 417–8
42-Year-Old Male, Merchant

For as has been indicated, *this* entity, this soul, is too precious in the eyes of the Creator that it should wantonly and without forethought leave off or get away from those basic influences and forces that do *innately* prompt these desires, these forces and influences for good to others.

Hence we find those turmoils that have arisen and that have become a part of the entity's experience at this time are in a manner that of fear and self-condemnation at times.

And to justify self has allowed self to be drawn into those environs and those attempts to substitute material things for that which may only be found in the *real* desire of the entity to "do good"—spirituality!

Hence the entity having left God out of consideration with the thought of material duty, and with that desire to fulfill that which is—to be sure—the material manifestation of good. Yet ye cannot gain good by doing that which condemns thine own self. Ye cannot do good through evil channels. Ye cannot do evil and expect good to continually come from same.

These are as attempting to gather figs from thistles, or grapes from bramble briars. These are not the natural forces. Neither are they such that have prompted and do prompt that expression, the desire to do good and to be good. That is not man's problem alone to be good, but to be good *for something*, to be good as a purposefulness! And these cannot be gained by the evil associations nor evil communications that make for the moments of satisfying either the material or the physical-mental desires in monetary gains.

Better that there be the crust alone of bread than the mansions of the millions with that of a condemning heart, a condemning spirit within self that there is a question mark after any activity, or any associations. For these are not God's ways, and thou hast *known* and thou dost know in thine heart of hearts the ways of good! Not that of long-facedness, not that of the saintly sinner, not that of the cynic; but doing good for Good's sake, doing good because it brings contentment, it brings harmony, it brings peace, it brings associations that create in the hearts of the associates *joy* and *hope* and the *longing* for the greater knowledge of the *source* of good. Not just good but *being*, acting, thinking in terms of that honest, due consideration for each and every individual, and not the advantage by chance, not the advantage by foreknowledge, not the advantage in any way or manner over thy fellow man.

For as in the manner ye treat thy fellow man ye treat thy Maker. And ye *cannot* do that which is questioning in thine own heart and soul to thy neighbor, to thy wife, to thy child, without it bringing turmoil, without it bringing discontent, without it bringing confusion. For these are the children of confusion, questioning thine own self.

Then, in what way, in what manner, where has the error been, how can the self find self?

Know first, the Lord thy God hath not tempted any soul, He hath not given any soul that it may not meet. And He hath prepared a way of escape for each soul if it will but harken to that voice deep *within!* Not through some long-winded individual's sayings, not that there will not be those inclinations to say, "Well, this or that or the other makes little or no difference," but that which is the prompting of the inner conscience.

For this *ye* know well, has tripped or whipped thee oft. *Ye* know well how there has come again and again that attempt to not face that ye know in thine own heart, by doing that which would for the moment— possibly—give the opportunities for monetary or material gains. But these take wings and ye curse thy luck. There is no luck—only God's service! For the earth is His and He will not *always* chide thee, neither will He always be longsuffering—lest *ye* show in thine own heart that ye are patient and longsuffering and can endure hardships, can endure those taunts and jeers of those who are worldlywise—yea, that may be in those positions of power through their own—as they call—material gains. But these, too, falter; these, too, fail. And only that thou hast deep in thy soul and conscience does last. And to live in life with a conscience that is continually dogging thee, continually warring against thine own better self in the desire to do good, is to indeed live in a hell fire itself.

And ye can, ye know the way! Turn about! Face thyself! Speak with

Him! For His promises have been, "When ye call *I will hear!*" No matter how far ye have gone. For ye may find Him. For if ye take wings and fly unto the uttermost parts of heaven, He is there! Though ye make thy bed in hell, He is there!

Then call and He will hear, and ye will know that there is greater satisfaction. For as indicated in the desire, there is the feeling, the knowledge of duty, of obligation, of those conditions that surround thee in the nature of thy own loved ones, those that make to thee life and its experiences worthwhile. And the fear of what others might say, thou hath failed in this, thou hath failed to keep this or that, has caused thee *oft* to do and to dodge thine own conscience . . .

Take that as has just been given to do first. First ye do not seek Morris or any firm, until thou hast determined within thine own heart that the whole program of thy life, thy associations, of thy wife, of thy son, is taken into consideration. And then, when this is done, and there is and there will come to thine experience that thou art indeed able and willing to do and dare—not merely for tomorrow's bread, not merely for tomorrow's security of thy son and thy wife, but for thy *God* and for thy love of good and for thy love of being not merely looked up to as being a good salesman, but good *for something* in those abilities!

And ye will find the way will *open!* Do not think ye can take short cuts. Oft these have been attempted. Too oft thine own good intentions have become the cobblestone to that of near self-destruction, to self-effacement, to that of "Damn the luck" that has brought so much of the spoiling of thy faith in thyself and in thy fellow man.

But if ye do these, then whether Morris Schwartz (for this is a good association or connection) or to others that open before thee, the way will come.

(Q) *Should I try and borrow some money to keep up my shoe business, or should I let it go?*

(A) When ye have made the connections, dispose of the shoe business. Cut thyself away from all of thine OLD associations or connections.

(Q) *What can I do to increase the sales at my shoe business long enough to build up my new business?*

(A) As we find, if there are those first things done first—first things done *first!* Then ye will find the way is opened and there is shown thee step by step. Not *only* the manner in which there may be the disposal of the shoe business to advantage, but the new associations, as the representative, become sufficient to care for all the needs and the good intentions—if the intentions are kept.

And may the blessings of the God that giveth thee life and hope sustain thee, ever!

2

●

Putting Material Things into Proper Perspective

Reading 3376–2
36–Year–Old Female, Stenographer

In any field of endeavor ye may succeed. What is needed in the present is concentration on what thy hands find to do. But know where you are going, and He will lead thee aright.

(*Q*) *What talents should I develop to achieve financial independence and greater happiness—now?*

(A) If that is what ye seek, beware. Let financial independence be the result rather than the cause of activity in any direction. For the silver and the gold are His. Put thyself into His hands. Use thy talents in directing people—the young, the old, the aged, the infirm, those that are weary, those that are full of life. Show them all the way, not so much by theory as by thy smile, thy gladness, thy happiness in knowing Him. And ye will find that the ways will open, whether it be in teaching, in ministering, in direction, or in any activity—for ye will find the way.

(*Q*) *Why am I not married at this time? Is there a spiritual lesson to learn and if not can I bring marriage into my experience, now?*

(A) You could have been married several times! In getting a little bit cynical you made them all afraid of you!

(*Q*) *Where should I look for employment and along what lines while I'm developing?*

(A) Right where you are! In any of the fields of activity ye choose, ye can excel—not just succeed but excel. Begin at the beginning, though; that is, within self. Ye will commence close to the top when you begin to act.

Reading 5469-1
Adult Female, Secretary

Edgar Cayce: Yes, we have the body, the enquiring mind, [5469], present in this room, and those surroundings and conditions in the life, mentally, physically, and materially. Ready for questions.

(Q) *Give advice to the body as to how she may regain peace and happiness, and sleep?*

(A) In considering this phase of the body, the *physical* must *also* be considered, as well as the mental and spiritual body; for there is the body–physical, the body–mental, the body–spiritual. Each manifesting in this material plane through the attributes of each in their, and in each particular, sphere. In the physical we find that of the material manifested conditions, and those conditions that worry and prevent happiness are produced often by the mental and spiritual outlook; for, as has so oft been given, the spirit is continually at war with the flesh. Will one satisfy only the desires of the flesh, then the mental and spiritual *must* suffer, and bring into being—through that suffering—those conditions that become as torment to the individual; for remember that it was said, truly, "though He were the Son, yet learned He obedience through the things which He suffered," and when an individual so attunes the mental, the spiritual life, as *not* to be in accord with that element within self that demands as much recognition as the purely material body, then one must know that there must be the price paid in that of discontent, of disruption, where faith becomes shaken, where there comes the falling of the idol of the eye, the shattering of hope, and that intenseness often reaches such conditions as to produce for the body that of sleeplessness, inability to control emotions, inability to control even circumstances and self's own will—that gift of the gods that makes mankind that as he is, that he may be either one with or away from His presence. In Him is peace, in His counsel is there faith, in His light and in the shelter of His wing is there to be found aid—mentally, physically, spiritually; for He is faithful who has given "Will ye be my people, I will be *your* God."

Then, as to how may this body find peace, find rest—again find in life and in life's associations—take counsel in *this*, that was said: "I go that ye may have a place, where I am, and what ye ask in *my* name, *believing*, *that* shall ye have", and in this way, and only in this counsel, may there come peace to *this* body—ye to *any* that be troubled in the flesh; for the flesh is weak, but the *spirit* is willing, and he—or she—that harkeneth to the voice from within, will find in Him that that brings contentment, a life *worth* living, a life *well* lived—joy in service; not that one, or that this body, need attempt to do that which is as *glory* to the Father, but in the little things that one may do to the fellowman, is lending to the Lord, who gives peace, who gives faith, who gives counsel, who gives all that is manifested in a material plane; for, as He hath given, "He that gives a cup of water in *my* name shall in no wise lose his reward."

To find that, then—so study to show self approved unto God, a workman being not ashamed; for He made Himself of no estate that we, through Him, might have that access to that throne of mercy, that fountain of joy, that place of peace, that rest in Him. This is not fanciful, but—tried in the life, brings that as is sought.

(Q) *How will the business affairs turn out, with which she is occupied? and when will relief come?*

(A) In this business, as there is the dependency upon many conditions in the affairs of many peoples, and not only in the relationships of individuals—but of states and nations. These have to do with forces as are of both economic and political relationships. There has already been set in motion those conditions through which the entity's, this body's endeavors, with the relationships as borne by same with others, will *enable* same to be carried forward again, even to a *better* position than has been occupied in the past. Those other connections necessarily will be made—*these* will be made possible also, and in the next changes as will come in the new shipments—and the connections as are being made—these will make for the material conditions as to be *much* more satisfactory.

First find thine own relation to thy Creator. Then may all these things be added unto you, for "the silver and the gold is *mine*, saith the Lord, and the cattle on a thousand hills. He that abideth in me shall not want; neither shall the desire of his heart go unrewarded."

(Q) How can the body get out of investments so as to cover her debts?

(A) These should be taken to one with whom the body may advise openly, and such investments as may be turned in the present to account, as to worthwhile, may be so changed and so turned as to be made able to cover, *recover* and add fourfold to that as already in sight. Fret not thyself against an evil day. Rather know that, that position thou occupiest is but to be used as stepping stones to greater things as may be accomplished in thine own present experience. Take these, then, to one who will harken and listen, who believes in the same sources through which *This* body seeks counsel, and there will come succor and aid in this direction. Go to [137]!

(Q) When will the conditions of the business improve so that the body may take out that which belongs to her?

(A) After the next changes, or in the early Fall.

(Q) What shall body do and what shall body not do?

(A) That depends upon the *relationship* as is contemplated, or as is brought about as regarding the changes the body will find coming into the life, into the experience, by the change of attitude the body must take as respecting self and as respecting others. *Do not* condemn others! *Do not* condemn *self!* Self-condemnation for that which is past, that which cannot be rectified, is but to heap reproach upon self. Reproach not self *nor* others, for that may be used in that as is to come for the *betterment of* self—mentally, spiritually, financially. Let thy yea's be yea's, and thy no's be no's. Learn when to say yea, and when to say nay. Make not the satisfying of selfish or fleshly desires, nor position nor fame, first and foremost; for the position as is occupied by self is even an *enviable* one by many. Then *do not* find fault. Rather make thine self at an at-*oneness* with the divine as is within, that it (the divine) may shine out through every act, every thought, of the body and the mind; for "Thoughts are deeds, and may become *miracles* or crimes." Act in that way and manner as to look *every man* in the face and tell him where to get off! knowing that the purpose and *will* is set in an *unchangeable* way *with* Him who is able to keep that committed unto Him against that day, whether materially, mentally, or spiritually.

(Q) *What shall body do about her family, in Europe, in order to get them settled into some business so they may be able to provide for themselves?*

(A) With the changes as are coming about, through the new relationships as are being established through the political and economical relationships, this may be brought about *sooner* than the body expects. This may be accomplished through those relationships as are soon to be established politically.

(Q) *What outside interests can the body find to give her peace?*

(A) Find the fellow that has less than self and give half thou hast to him! That only as an illustration, to be sure, but *interest* self in—*not* as a social worker, *not* as a missionary! Rather as an interest in the fellow-man because he, or she, is one *with* thine own self, and a *manifestation* of the might of the God thou would worship!

Reading 5713–1
42–Year–Old Male, Merchant

(Q) *Any further advice?*

(A) Much may be given the body as the directing of self and of the relationships with others, as respecting conditions whether of the material, social, or business relations. Well would the body consider this as a real truth in the life, and life's experience and associations: Let the business or monetary prosperity be the *outcome* and not the *end* of thine endeavors; for those that would develop for self and have of this world's goods must make self in accord with those elements that bring such conditions, and these *cannot* be accomplished with success rather than that as will *produce* success first and foremost in the mind. We are through for the present.

Reading 232–2
72–Year–Old Female

As to the financial, in this we find there has been and is some distress to the mental faculties of the entity. These we find will in the early fall adjust themselves to the needs, wishes and desires of this entity. Let this mind be kept ever in the mental forces of this entity, that the best comes to him, or her, who serves best.

Reading 1929–1
41–Year–Old Female. Husband was contemplating accepting a new job offer and relocating his family

(Q) *What particular thing am I best fitted to do?*

(A) To be a teacher by precept and example to those that would seek to know His way, as they go up to the holy city, or as they seek His face.

(Q) *My husband is contemplating giving up his job and going to Washington, D.C. Would it be wise to do so? Please advise me.*

(A) As is felt innately in self, through those manners or ways that have been indicated, this would be unwise in the present; until there are changes in conditions or circumstances, both for self and for those that would be influenced by such a change in the present.

(Q) *Where may I look for a better job?*

(A) As indicated by that first given, by the middle of the present month we find there shall be many changes imminent in the experience of the entity mentally; and the mental being the builder, naturally there will gradually come about those influences that will offer greater opportunities. Do not be too hasty in the present, but rather let these grow as those things that are the outcome of an experiencing of self in His hands, His ways, His directions.

(Q) *I have cares and obligations. How can these be best met?*

(A) These are met step by step, as the spiritual life would direct self. Know that the cares and the obligations are those that make for the balancing of self, and know that these will be cared for in the way and manner as He sees, would self entrust self's activities in His ways and manners.

Reading 2135–1
48–Year–Old Widow. Woman very concerned about her finances

In entering this present experience, as we find, the entity comes under the astrological influence of Mercury—afflicted with Saturn; Jupiter and Venus, also affliction in Saturn—with a benevolent influence in Uranus and Neptune. These, as we find, have made in this present experience rather unusual circumstances in the life of the entity. With the high mental development, with the aptitudes as experienced in the early portion of gathering from the associations, surroundings and studies, much of a nature that made for the entity an exceptional body among groups and individuals, in its social and its mental and material life. In the changes brought, there has come the fear of the conditions in the financial position, as well as bounty in these directions. As a promise in the associations in the filial and home life, as well as those that have brought heartaches, yearnings and longings that have reached in the *present* circumstances, conditions and surroundings, that as of almost unbearable conditions. As has been seen, as will be experienced by the entity through those activities of the body–mental, the soul development of the entity, these in *many* ways *have* been, were, necessary—that there be the proper understanding of relationships and the proper *valuation in* the life, in the soul, of those things in a material life that may be made as the criterions; for, as is experienced, as *has* been experienced in the present, those things—while they may be in a manner that bring contentment, or a satisfaction rather in the material things of life . . . takes wings and there is naught but to rely on that promise as has been made to mankind, womankind, since the foundations of the earth, "Will ye abide *in* Me, I will abide in you." Take little thought of those things that are but of today. Knowest thou not that, art thou in that way of being a light to few or many in *His* way, that He will preserve thee against every opposition? against thine enemies, against the things evil spoken of, against those conditions that thou art seemingly unable to center as this or that? but *keep* the heart in accord with that thou knowest. As thou gained in the first portion of the experience, and in the developments as the budding into the womanhood, with those same thoughts, those same ideals, keep those trusts that thou knowest are true! Be not unmindful that, art thou in HIS keeping, He will not allow thee to be tempted beyond that ye are *able* to bear. Doth He not clothe the sparrow and the lily alike? Doth He not provide for those of *His* creatures? Be thou rather in the hands of the *living* God, than in the hands of those who speak lightly of the things thou wouldst do!

Reading 2927–1
50–Year–Old Male. Individual was interested in a life reading and, among other things, his life's mission

Thus the admonition to this entity:

The purpose of one's entrance to a material plane is not for the gratifying of self alone but for the contribution such an entity, or each entity,
may make to the glorifying of the sources of spiritual and mental application of the basic truth.

Thus may the attaining to the material things be the better or greater
accomplishment of an individual entity.

The acknowledgement of this, deep and latent in self, may be termed
the basis of the entity's success in this material sojourn.

The greater this is magnified, then, in the dealings with the fellow
man, the greater may be the material gains and the satisfaction gained
in its labors by the entity.

That this is to be accomplished for an ideal, or in meeting an ideal,
should then be the greater purpose of this entity.

Reading 2896–1
22–Year–Old Male, Journalist

One that is especially gifted in the affairs of peoples, rather than of
things or figures; or data *concerning* things and people, rather than that
of statistics as numbers, or such; yet these will always influence the
activities *of* the entity—that is, statistics, figures—but will the entity attune self to those of the mental and *spiritual* forces from within, and
gain *for* self that of the ability to commune with self and those seeking
aid, those from whom the entity would seek such contributions for the
aid of the many, the *spirit* will bring those influences as will direct for
the *successful* life in the present experience, so far as *fame* and fortune are
concerned.

As to whether the entity will have, *after* the fifty–sixth year, that feeling of the life being worth *while*—this will depend upon the *application* of
self as respecting the various influences as will come to the entity.

In days, weeks, years—the entity will find that those that are divisible
by numbers with ciphers will ever bring a change, as has been seen. The
first, the tenth, the twentieth, and the thirtieth—these will bring *changes*
in the experience, in the relationships, in the environment. As to what
these *do* to the *entity*, is the *entity's* self! As to what the entity does *for* and
to the various changes is what the entity should worry—if it's termed
worry; at least *exercise* self most as concerning. *Not*, then—"What I may

gain *from*"—but "What may I give *to* the ones whom I contact, whom I may be associated *with*"—should *be* the attitude of the entity.

Reading 779–19
43–Year–Old Male, Unemployed Marble Cutter, Monument Salesman

Gertrude Cayce: You will have before you the body and the enquiring mind of [779], ..., Ala. You will also have before you the information as has been given this body in previous *life, business* and *physical* readings. Also you will have before you his family–home life and all of the conditions and circumstances that surround this body and his family. You will also have before you his financial condition and the lack of employment and the immediate need of aid and employment whereby he can meet the necessary obligations and needs of life for himself and family. In view of all these facts you will please tell this body in full detail what is the proper and correct method to proceed under the existing conditions and circumstances to get employment of some kind, even if it is not in his regular line of work, whereby he can meet the necessary obligations and needs of life for himself and those dependent upon him. Please advise as to with whom, how, where and when may he expect to be able to make a permanent connection with success and contentment for himself and family.

Edgar Cayce: Yes, we have the body, the enquiring mind, [779]—this we have had before—also the information as has been given the body, the various circumstances, conditions as confront the body.

In the conditions, in the circumstances and the surroundings as does appear those conditions that to the body have become in some manners apparently unsurmountable, or that as has been rather the continued lack of ability to cope with, to meet the needs to carry on in the manner as *seemeth* befitting to the body from that as has been experienced in the past by the body—in considering all circumstances, all surroundings, the body, the enquiring mind, the mental forces of the body should take in consideration that as has been and is necessary for the mental being, the soul development, to meet that which has been meted by the body; and that will the body keep that faith, that hope in that power wherein the sources of all things come—whether of the material, the mental or the soul forces—*their* emanations, their activities must come from the One Source, and that doing that as is understood from day to day will bring that necessary understanding for the body, the mind, the mental, the physical being, to bring that as is necessary to meet any and every emergency that may arise. The trials may be considered hard, judged by the surroundings of many. Judge *not* as to what is to be meted for the understanding; rather how soon will the self get the proper understanding.

In meeting the emergencies and those conditions in the present, as has been outlined for the body, there are specific lines in which the body may excel. That, then, should be in the direction in which the body should take for the immediate needs, through those channels where the supply for those of household necessities, whether in those of that used from day to day, those in cleaning, those in brushing, those in home remedies, or in any of those fields may the body meet those emergencies *of* the present. As the application of self is made in these directions, may the body gain that necessary understanding and association as to bring about that which will make *for* the development *of* self and those dependent upon same. Do that.

Reading 1861–2
33–Year–Old Male, Music Teacher

(Q) *Should I marry the girl [2072] to whom I am engaged?*

(A) As we find, if the ideals of each are compatible, it may be made to be an experience worthy of acceptation.

(Q) *What can I do to insure my economic future and what line of work should I follow, and how shall I proceed if I am to change from what I am now doing?*

(A) As has been indicated, the field of service lies in music—or music as combined with the application of high vibrations to human ills.

Teaching—or practicing—or giving to others the greater concept of the purposes of music in their experience—is the way and manner to insure not only economic force and power, but mental and spiritual development.

Let the economic power, however, be *not* the first cause; let it rather be the *result* of careful, purposeful consideration of the use of abilities given to each entity, each soul—and be the *result* of such application.

(Q) Would you advise a change from what I am now doing?

(A) Not in the immediate. Let this come rather as an after effect of better physical and mental and *spiritual* abilities being developed within the purposeful life.

Reading 348–14
48–Year–Old Salesman

In the abilities of the entity and that to which it may attain in the present, and how:

As has been seen, there are things, are conditions—both mental, material and spiritual—upon which the entity should put *much* thought, and know in whom thou hast believed, and that He is able to keep that committed *unto* thee, as *thou* wilt serve Him! Then, knowing the abilities, the fields of activities, that give self the opportunity to serve, *use* those *in* a way that will bring self's understanding, and the *material* results, the physical results, are in His keeping; for never has he that served the living God *wanted* for the necessities of life. Consider the lilies, how they grow; they toil not, neither do they spin; yet they are supplied even as those of *all* creation, that are *used*—and do not *abuse*—God's privileges.

Reading 1152–2
61–Year–Old Writer, Widow

(Q) Should any physical applications be made to benefit my health, or is the clearing of my thoughts sufficient at all times?

(A) This, in the light of the consciousness of the mind of this entity, is well to be considered from the same angles as He, the Healer, presented.

In each individual case we find Him presenting that in the consciousness of the individuals to create in *their* consciousness the whole concept of life, light, and its relationships to the material effects to be created in the minds of those to whom He would give health, life and understanding.

Each individual entity, then, presents—from that angle—an individual problem. And there are those experiences in the consciousness of every entity needing the purer clarification.

As we find with this entity, there needs be that induction of the activities within the body that would assist in re-ionizing or re-vitalizing the whole of the body–being. Not that there is to be the laying aside of *any* of the consciousness of the divine supplying the whole necessary for the sustenance of the physical or the mental or the spiritual bodies . . .

(Q) *Regarding the situation which has arisen between the friend who went abroad with me and myself. Please explain this, and how I can meet it.*

(A) These conditions arise from former differences of opinion. And there has been gradually builded an antagonism that may only be melted with loving indifference.

This, to be sure, at first may be called contradictory. For how *can* there be *loving* indifference?

How gave He, thy pattern?

When there arose those experiences when others were called to His presence and they said, "See, these in thy name heal the sick, cast out demons, yet they gather not with us. Rebuke them." But what was His answer? "Nay; nay, not so—for they that gather not with us scatter abroad the praises. Leave them, lest they turn again upon *you* and use that thou hast done to thine own confusion." [Paraphrasing of Matt. 9:49, 50; Luke 11:23; Matt. 7:6.]

Then thy attitude should be:

"Lord, they are thine, as I am thine. I am willing. I forgive. I present the problems to thee. Use me, use them, in whatever may be Thy will in the matter."

This then puts thee in that position that there is no stumblingblock, and that becomes then *loving* indifference. For ye have left it in the hands of the Creator, who alone can give life and withdraw it.

(Q) *What is the cause of such an attitude?*

(A) As has just been indicated.

(Q) *Regarding material affairs: My property in Cleveland, Ohio—have my decisions regarding same been correct?*

(A) These have been doubtful within self. Then it becomes rather confusing.

But this is the manner in which each individual should weigh such matters, and this applies to self:

Mind in the flesh or in materiality is for the purpose of the manifestations of God's love to the children of men. "Thou will, then, O God, in my meditations, in my seeking, *guide* me in the use of that thou hast lent to me as thy servant, thy child, thy loved one; that it may be used in the proper way and manner."

And ye say ye believe. Then know that what is given thee in such meditations is in keeping with His will, and ye would not have it otherwise.

Reading 5332–1
58–Year–Old Male, Automotive Engineer, U.S. Army

In analyzing same there is much to be considered and here the entity is seeking much that it doesn't expect, doesn't give full credence in, and yet know that within self ye are an individual entity, a universe within self, with all the potential powers and faculties of the divine, as well as the hellish. And these ye may manifest through thy own will.

The entity must find in self, if it would accomplish more, the ability to open the hand to give out; and in the giving out may ye receive. For that which is of the spiritual, in giving ye receive. For it is as of love, of friendship, of those which are ever Creative; they grow within themselves by doing, and when it becomes as something it would close away from others, it becomes as something that would deteriorate within its own self.

Thus the entity is a capable individual, one given to scientific analysis, scientific study, the reasons for same; but the advancements, if the entity would find same, must be by giving.

Oft the entity listens; yes, too good a listener for its own good. For as the entity listens, it may oft turn the conversation into channels which would be much more inspiring and much more helpful, but because of that little streak of selfishness, it refrains and thus oft loses opportunities. There are these influences the body should analyze and find: there is the body–physical, there is the body–mental and there is the body–spiritual. The spirituality, then, of self is expressed in the individuality of the entity and this is at times indicated. As has just been given, know what thy ideal is spiritually, mentally, materially. And then go about to practice same. For to know to do good, and to do it not, it is sin to that soul; and to know the manner in which ye may help others and refrain, it is hellish in thine own self, creating conditions which must be antagonistic in thine own experience with others. It is the law of grace and the law of recompense, the law of love.

Seek, then, first the Lord while He may be found and all others of the material, of the mental will be added in their proper place, their proper relationships.

Reading 4113-1
Adult Female. Seeking mental and spiritual advice:

(Q) *What should the body do to successfully handle her present and future invest-ments?*

(A) Study to show self approved unto God, the *giver* of all good and perfect gifts; knowing that, that held in this world's goods is lent of the Lord *to* those *with* the ability *to* apply same *in* a direction that will make manifest His love for the peoples through whom the entity *may* contact.

(Q) *What banker would be a good adviser for this body in whom she could have implicit trust?*

(A) This may be sought best through the mental forces of the body. Contacts have been made. Associations are already in line. As long as they show themselves trustworthy—if you would be trusted, trust an-other. If you would have friends, show one's self friendly. If you would have abilities, apply that you already have in hand.

(Q) *Please advise body how to get the most help and hope from her occult associa-tion?*

(A) By entering into the silence at least once each day, and applying self in the use of that as is already known, felt, has been experienced by self, may be experienced by self; knowing that the spirit from within will counsel with, and guide—and study self first.

(Q) *What branch of social work would best assist body to use her time to best advantage?*

(A) Do as has been given! Try *That! Then* we may give further.

Reading 541-1
47-Year-Old Female, Widow:

As each soul enters in the earth, there are purposes other than that which may be arising from desire of those that physically are respon-sible for such an advent.

For, the soul seeks from the realm of spirituality to give expression of that it as an entity or soul may do with its experiences in the mental realm, as well as about that it *has* done in a physical realm.

Hence the law that is ever present; like attracts like; like begets like. Hence there is the attraction as from the desires of those in the physical calling to the sources of generation in the flesh, to the sources of creation or of spirit in the spiritual realm.

Hence there is often a real purpose in the soul, as in this soul, seeking a period of expression of self; and finding it in that about the bodies when there is the period of presentation. For, while the physical begins at conception, the spiritual and mental is as the first breath taken into the physical—that becomes then a living soul, with a physical organism for manifestation during the sojourn in that particular experience . . .

So, the entity here finds these as attributes in the mental forces that lie—as it were—*dormant* or innate in each soul or body manifested in the earth, that may be *drawn upon* when apparently everything else has failed. That stamina of character, that indwelling which is a portion of the soul. That which makes for the abilities of each soul to draw nigh unto him that *is* light, life, and from or through that source build—in and under all circumstances—that which makes for beauty to any who may behold such a soul's activity; and most of all bring to the soul harmony even under oppression or subjugation by circumstances of a material nature, and beauty and joy to those who may contact such an individual or soul. Becoming a light to many, a pathway that may guide many—even as this entity ... the ability to hold to that hope—and this increased in the knowledge of Him that is light—may bring yet joy and peace and harmony that makes for being content in that place one finds self, and knowing that He may have His way with thee. Making for the ability of great expansion of *subjects*; the ability to read and to comprehend much that is not seen by others who may be reading or studying in the same class or group. The natural abilities of a leader, yet the entity is often burdened by the fact that so many apparently are always depending upon what little resources the entity has from the material standpoint. The entity should declare in self those forces that are ever present, that the supply is of such a nature that it may never diminish as long as there is the holding to the power in His name....

Also there are the abilities to meet with the varied groups that are often drawn into the experiences of the entity for their edification, for their enlightenment; and be ever ready to give the reason for the faith that lies within thine inner self and thine inner consciousness. Know from the earthly viewpoint a reason; whether it answers to thy neighbor or thy friend, *that* is for thine self! For, thine own soul seeks expression; and if it satisfies in thee, then *live it!* not in a selfish manner, but as expressing that which may bring to self, to others, first of all *contentment*; for upon this is peace, harmony, happiness attained...

And may bring for the entity through such associations and relations, even in the material as well as the mental plane, those things that will be the more helpful and aidful to bringing joy and happiness in the present experience . . .

As to the abilities, then, in the present, and that to which the entity may attain and how:

From that intimated and given, it is indicated that by turning to those influences that are ever about the self for aid, help may come; whether it be in the abilities for the compilation of those things that may be of help or what not. (Send them to Silver, Burdette & Company!) This will bring to the body the greater blessings in the material things, and will bring for those whom the body seeks to aid through such channels those things that will make for this experience being a development.

Be kind to self, to others. Keep the way ever open; for He would walk and talk with thee oft, wilt thou but open thine self and be the channel.

Reading 4046–1
32–Year–Old Female, Stenographer

We find also the urge in Neptune to be associated with those things, people, places having to do with water. Water is the mother of materiality. Don't let materiality and material things, then, be put first and foremost in thy experience. That is the next warning. Don't let material things supplant spiritual things, but know that the material things should be a result of entertaining the spiritual forces, the creative energies and activities, and the mental application should be to coordinate and cooperate with the efforts of spiritual purposes and ideals to bring material results in the experience of the entity.

Reading 5752-2-1
Requested by Edgar Cayce on the topic of a lecture he planned to give on "How to Develop Your Psychic Powers"

How best, then, to develop those latent forces in one *now*, those who have reached the years of maturity or responsibility in self? Let that mind be in you as was in Him who thought it not robbery to make Himself equal with God, yet took on Himself the burden of all that through His physical suffering, His privation in body, in mind, there might come the blessings to others. Not self, but others. He, or she, that may lose self, then, for others, may *develop* those faculties that will give the greater expression of psychic forces in their experience.

What shall I read? Wherewithal shall I be clothed? Where shall I dwell? What shall I eat? and the like, become the questions of many. He that taketh thought of such has *already* limited the powers that influence through those forces in life. The *natural* things, as known and given, are the things that make for the better physical body in normal activity. *Normalcy*, not extreme in any manner! and there will be shown thee day by day that which will be the necessary for thine *own* development. To some certain amount of exercise, certain amounts of rest, certain amounts of various characters of breathing, of purification, of prayer, of reading—as is found necessary; but of *all* be true to that thou promiseth that source from which all health, all aid, must come! Don't fool yourself; for you *cannot* fool your Maker, and if there is fooling it is yourself—for your brother will soon find you out!

Reading 3179-1
53-Year-Old Female

(Q) *Would I do well to continue with my music?*

(A) It is that which spans the distance between the sublime and the ridiculous, between the finite and the infinite. Keep the music, for it is oft a help to thee to quell the storms of life.

(Q) *Will I find another companion or will I earn my own living the rest of my days?*

(A) Whose is the silver and the gold of the earth? Earn same rather by living such a life that He may lend to thee. For those who are endowed with worldly goods are debtors indeed to the Divine. The misuse of same is that that leadeth to the hard way. For, as has been given, straight and narrow is the way. Those that seek Him may find it, but it is hard for those that possess this world's goods to give it to the poor, and yet such are the poorer of the two.

As to whether a companion—depends upon what is thy ideal. What is His law pertaining to same? Rather live that He may lend to thee indeed.

Reading 5665–1
46–Year–Old Male, Merchant. Individual interested in questions regarding business, financial associations, and all phases of life

(Q) Shall he go in business for himself?

(A) In this direction we would first make the proper associations and connections, and *later* launch in business for self.

(Q) Advise the body when and how he can regain the financial loss he has sustained?

(A) This dependent upon *how* the body would desire to regain such. One, in considering one's position and one's relations to their fellow man and to the world, as well as to self, should first make for self and for self's purposes, self's desires, that position which fully, loyally, wholly and wholly prepares, fits, and makes for that position desired, as one that *should* be *entitled to* those conditions, those surroundings, those environs, those things that make for *that* desired, and not only *in* the light of self's own esteem—for he that esteemeth himself to be something when he is not is an unwise servant, but he that lendeth himself in aid, in help, in understanding to his fellow *man*, lendeth to the Lord, and "I will repay, saith the Lord of hosts". Use that thou hast in hand, in understanding self and self's relation to thine fellow man, and thine relation to the Creator in THIS thy present position, and he that calleth and he that harkeneth to my ways will not be deserted, saith the Lord. Keep thine own skirts clean. Keep thine hands *free* from those things that bespeak of *uncleanness*. Be not afraid to meet the word or the act in *any* company, in *any* position, and that position as is best for self and self's development will *be* thine heritage. Be *content* in the place ye find yourselves, but be satisfied only in well doing.

(Q) What can he do to secure peace and happiness?

(A) Follow that as has just been given.

(Q) *Any further advice regarding—*

(A) Know thyself, thy weaknesses, thy faults, and find in Him that giveth knowledge to him that seeketh, the answer to the needs of the mind, the body, the soul; for he that harkeneth, he that knocketh, he that seeketh, will not go unrepaid. We are through for the present.

Reading 1362–1
48–Year–Old Male, Executive Assistant

Thy field of service to thy fellow men, as has been indicated, becomes in the fields of communication; that deal with the radio and every form of communication; and a closer association with the national and international fields of operative forces will bring thee greater happiness in *lending* of thyself, for it becomes a portion of thyself—and will make for an outlet where the material gains may come.

But first *know* ye the Lord, for the cattle and the gold and the silver are His, and all ye have is lent ye of the Lord! Only that ye give away, of self, of money, of time, of patience, of love, do ye possess!

For if ye would have life, give life! If ye would have friends, *be* friendly! If ye would have loved ones, love others, do good to them though they may despitefully use you; for they did that unto thy Lord and Master.

In the application of self in the fields of activity, draw nigh unto that which is good and it will draw nigh unto thee.

Ready for questions.

(Q) *Please advise me as to the present stability of my position with the ... Electric Co. Is there an opportunity to realize a satisfactory future there, or should I make a change?*

(A) As we find, as has been indicated, this has been and may be used as a stepping–stone to greater opportunities, greater possibilities for the associations with communication fields rather than those of *commercial* lines in the electrical forces—that offer the greater opportunities. And ways and means are being opened that as we find will bring about an association of that nature.

For soon, as has been so oft given from here, there must be a closer association with the telegraph, the radio and the telephone communications.

Hence as all of these have been through the many ages, through the many experiences of this entity, this soul, thy study, thy desire, thy wishes, thy activity—to give expression in same in the present offers the greater opportunities for advancement materially. But in thine advancement let this warning be:

Think not only of material gains, but of how great a service ye may be to thy fellow man! For if ye serve the masses, the individuals, without thought of self save as for service, ye serve thy Maker.

(Q) Having desired to be re-associated with [...] with whom I was previously connected, when and how should I best continue my negotiations and contacts with [...]?

(A) As has been indicated, there are—as we find—those conditions being brought about in which there may be closer and better associations; and in the application of self greater opportunities. As to how soon, keep those negotiations open—and prepare self, in thought, in body, in mind, for ready, active service in same.

(Q) How can I best adjust my upset financial affairs due to the depression?

(A) Just as has been indicated again, go to those whom thou owest obligations—and those things that materially demand consideration. Give the explanation, give the thought to same. *Ask* and ye will receive the opportunities for being able to meet them in thy service for others.

Not speculating, not calling on advantageous positions that ye would clear self; but know, only they that are able to suffer are able to know glory, to know peace, to know harmony. These may sound at first only as idealistic sayings, but if ye turn within and ask of thy better self ye will find the answer there.

(Q) Would it be possible to negotiate some loan whereby these obligations can be pooled, rather than all mixed up?

(A) As we find, as soon as there is definite (and permanent) connection made with communications, this very condition *can* be consummated and give self the opportunity to meet same in a way and manner that would be satisfactory to all.

Reading 2895–1
45–Year–Old Male. This was a life reading in which past–life influences on the present were discussed

In the one before this, in the days of the first upbuilding in the

Atlantean country. The entity then again in power, and among the chosen ones of the time, in the name Ishmeuel (as it would be in this language), and the entity both gained and lost, for the periods of advancement were such that much required, and much gained and lost in same. The urge from same, being that ever questionableness to self, as to whether the judgement of the entity correct or not; and the abilities, then, lie in that of the manufacturing end of products of the earth, and, as given, in same will the entity find the greatest success in the present sphere; the greater opportunities being presented to same during the latter part of the present year. Take advantage, then, of same; but build first in self that knowledge of the relations self, in the earth plane, bears to the Giver of all good and perfect gifts, knowing that when one has fully found the manifestations of the spirit of glory within, many more of those conditions that are necessary for the earthly sojourn will be added, through their natural means, to the entity.

Reading 1295–1
39–Year–Old Female. This was a health reading dealing with cancer

(Q) *Regarding the problem which disturbs me and hinders my health: Would you advise that we further reduce our standard of living, for greater security in the future?*

(A) This, to be sure, depends upon much of that as is the standard or the ideal. To be sure, that there is caused anxiety and worry, or the ideal. To be sure, that there is caused anxiety and worry, which acting upon the nervous system increases the activity of the pressures—that, as has been indicated, are sympathetic in nature; then we would not reduce to *such* a level that we worry from the other angle also.

For *all* help, all health, all source of supply is from the *divine* within. From those activities then of the mental self hold fast to that; then leave the results with Him. This will bring a consciousness of the divine purposes in all things that will create the greater harmony mentally, physically, spiritually.

(Q) *Any further advice for this body at this time?*

(A) Hold fast to self, not as self but as the opportunities as a channel, as an aid to those in the environs and the surroundings; and we will find these attitudes make for and build within the whole of the bodily functions the greater outlook for hopefulness, helpfulness in every way.

Reading 2842–2
38-Year-Old Female

(Q) *Have I a right to demand abundance, or should I be content with my small income?*

(A) Be *content* with what thou hast, but never be *satisfied* with what thou hast. Abundance is the lot of him who is in accord with those truths of the Creative Energy, just as the world—the hills, the cattle, the gold—is mine, sayeth the Lord. I will repay, sayeth the Lord. Put thine self in that attitude, that position, of reflecting that as is of the Creative Energy, and that necessary—and over an abundance will be in thine hand.

Reading 498–1
Adult Female

(Q) *What would be the most harmonious and remunerative business for me?*

(A) First we would make for the conditions that have been indicated, that a strong, healthy, well-balanced physical body may find, with its activities to make for same, a budgeting of its efforts in mental and physical and spiritual things, will find within itself—as it adjusts itself—those fields of activities presented to itself, so that when it is in a normal reaction it may proceed in that it has chosen—or as may have been pointed out to self through these very activities in bringing *health*; for with health may come wealth if it is needed in that for the spiritual development.

Would that most people would gain that knowledge that if they are attempting to live a normal life, if wealth is necessary for their soul development it is a portion of their experience!

(Q) *Will you give a prayer for meditation for this body?*

(A) **May there be done in me and through me that which the Lord seest I have need of, that I in His way may be of the greater service and the greater channel of blessings to others. Use me, in the name of the Father, of the Son, in the way though seest best.**

Reading 2409–1
47–Year–Old Male, Sales Executive

In Jupiter we find the universal consciousness, the adaptability to things as well as to groups and masses. Hence we will find the greater activities of the entity in the material plane will be with groups, but having individual application—as in the interests in education, in the activities that build home and its environs. And, as will be indicated by the experience of the entity in the material sojourns, if this interest and application will be kept ever in that way of seeking not merely material gains but the purpose first and foremost that such associations may be of a constructive nature in the experience of such groups and such individuals, we will find the entity being successful in all of its under-takings. Not that headaches, not that disturbing forces do not arise, but that *in* that influence the entity has the ability to *ever* hold the thought (and should) of constructive forces for the home building, rather than for material gains only for self.

For, know—as is the divine, the spiritual law—*man* may plan, man may sow the seed, but only *God* can and does give the increase.

So in thy dealings with thy fellow men, let those purposes ever be such that ye may meet them face to face always and know that thou hast taken thought of others...

Ready for questions.

(Q) Am I in the type of work that is best suited for my preparation and nature?

(A) Well—if it is applied in the manners indicated.

(Q) In what field of endeavor am I most likely to succeed financially?

(A) Read what has been given here, and leave off "financially." Let the financial be the result of honest, sincere desire to be and to live so that *others* may know the way also. *God* giveth the increase.

(Q) Are my present employers those with whom I should permanently associate?

(A) The original were thy employers before. You find them quite hard to deal with at times; *driving*, as it were, yet even thine own service has softened them much. Very well—for both.

(Q) Are there any disturbing factors in my business associations?

(A) Of the nature as indicated are the only ones we find.

(Q) Are my investments properly made?

(A) Analyze them in those manners and ways that have been here pointed out. These will prove the way to judge same. If they are for increase only, without honest service given, you'd better change them. If they are those that God Himself may smile upon, invest all the more!

(Q) *Is my desire to accumulate wealth in order to render service to humanity a laudable one?*

(A) A laudable one; but do not put the cart before the horse! For, if one cannot render service through his income will barely keep body and soul together, even if it were tripled or multiplied by a million he would not do any better!

Thus—use, practice that ye profess to preach.

3

●

The Importance of Ideals and Faith When Working with Financial Issues

Reading 3653-1
28-Year-Old Female

(Q) How can I best help my family financially?

(A) This will depend upon what the needs are. There is much more important help to the family than financial. If this is put first and foremost, ye may lose the way. If the ideal is set first, the finances will follow.

(Q) Any further advice to help my present needs?

(A) Begin at the beginning. Learn the way of love. "For the earth is the Lord's, and the fulness thereof."

Reading 1499-1
50-Year-Old Female

Hence all the more there is the necessity that the entity within self find what is its ideal. Not only in what it may believe, as for moral, religious, social or business associations and activities, but as to *Who* is the author of such a choice. Is it founded in a growth from within as of a spiritual nature, or is it founded in self-indulgence or self-gratification, or self-glorification?

For indeed if these last be the aims, the purposes in self, they must eventually turn upon thee. But if the seeds and the purposes are of truth, and knowledge pertaining to the spiritual associations in the activities–these being the cause, the purpose, yea the very author of thy faith, thy confidence, thy desire–then we may expect and we may know these will grow and bring the fruits of the spirit; enabling each soul to become more patient, more longsuffering, more charitable; with stronger fellowships and the abilities to know, though the world may be against thee, though there may be trials and tribulations, there may be even want in body and want in the material things for the body, yet that food which is found in Him as the author and finisher of thy faith becomes the bread of life, the water of life, the true vine–that is, the Son.

Then we may know all these things in their place and their purpose for the sustenance of the body and mind and soul *will* be supplied; if ye put thy whole trust in Him.

For indeed He is the Creator, He indeed is the Maker of all that doth appear. For all power in heaven and in earth has been given into His keeping through the faith He kept with His fellowman; by His advent into the earth, by His doing good in all ways, at all times, under every circumstance. Yet not railing, on any–though they demanded His life in the material, though they cuffed and buffeted Him, though they swore and spit upon him, though they crowned him with thorns, though they abased him in every manner, yet opened He not His mouth–though He were their Lord, their Master.

And as ye hold to Him, ye–too–may become lord and master of *every* situation in the material, in the mental, yea in the spiritual experiences through which ye may be called to pass.

For He hath indeed given His angels charge concerning thee. He hath promised indeed, "When ye call I will *hear*–and answer speedily." Yea, He hath given, "Try me"–but purge thyself of lust of every nature that ye may indeed know that peace as He gave, "My peace I leave with thee; not as the world counteth peace but as the Lord of love, of grace, of mercy." *These* be that peace that bringeth gladness and joy to the heart to be counted to be worthy to know His love in thy experience day by day.

Reading 5616–1
Adult Male

(Q) *Will my personal financial condition improve—when—how can I quickly lessen within reason the load of personal debts—should I try to make money outside of ... Co? If so, how?*

(A) This condition in itself opens many of the troublesome things to the body, both physical and mental, as well as filial relations. While they in the various phases present that which the body in *itself* would at times deny, yet in the background these are ever present in the mental, in the physical, and in the social relations. There are many fields through which the body—with its abilities—may add that of financial gain. The assumed obligations, the assumed financial relations, while they present at times a burden to the body, *mentally* (necessarily physically), yet these are not of such a nature, other than they often keep the better balance for the body's material and the body's mental development. Do not make haste other than slowly in gaining the perfect understanding of the purpose of life in this mundane sphere; for while it should be the *ideal* of every individual to succeed—and gain in understanding in the relationship of self with individuals—fame and fortune often take wings unless same are the *result* and not the *end* of a life spent in understanding what life's all about! There are coming to the body mentally and physically, from day to day, opportunities through which there might be gains made in material sense, quickly—yet these are not all of such a nature as to even be appealing to the sensibilities of the body; but do not pass all of these up without due consideration. We *find* there will be presented, in the week of May the 15th to the 22nd, an opportunity through which the body may assist self financially and materially in a way and manner that there is not a question mark after same. Do not so act in *any* manner—even though the burden may appear heavy—that the self's own conscience is questioning self. These, then, would be the better opportunities for the body.

Reading 877–29
48–Year–Old Male, Corporate Lawyer

(Q) *I seek direction as to how to clear my debts.*

(A) These can be met only by measuring up to that which brings the promise–that is well known in self–from the *sources* of supply–materially, physically.

For the earth is indeed the Lord's, and the fulness thereof. The silver and the gold are his.

When ye measure to that standard where there is needed such for the best mental and soul development, such is–will be–supplied.

(Q) My one and only desire is to do the will of our Father. What is His will for me?

(A) As has been given of old, know that it is not that someone–either from heaven or from over the seas–would bring thee a message, a direction. For it is within thine own self alone that the contact can me made.

Reading 900–61
30–Year–Old Male, Stockbroker

(Q) From what source, stocks, or my present business or outside will the finances come?

(A) This should be sufficient for the entity, that they, the finances, will come and that should suffice the entity to press on and do those things and in the manner that makes the reception of such finances meritorious to the individual, for as given, through these months, at this time, there comes the opportunity, the position, the conditions necessary for sufficient of this world's goods. Take advantage of same and be worthy of that trust. These we find will come through the channels in which the entity labors, provided that the entity keeps that faith, that way in which has been set, for all shall be considered, as has been given, in the entity's development, in the moral relation, in the business relation. That merited by the entity will be given. Some through stocks, some through other associations. Some through social, some through conditions that arise in other channels.

(Q) Am I following in the proper channel to bring about this financial opportunity?

(A) Very good. There are times, have been times, when there was lack of faith. These overcome. The entity understands, knows, feels the conditions. Keep self in the right channel, that they may be guided aright.

(Q) Am I pursuing the proper business methods to bring that financial remuneration?

(A) This is to be seen as yet, for the changes in policies, in manner, in way of conducting business relations are upon the entity at this time. Follow in the ways that have been set and that the entity knows and understands.

(Q) What will the opportunity be?

(A) To do the right.

(Q) Is there anything I may now do to speed it into realization?

(A) Keeping in that way that brings the best to the entity, for as was given of old, "The silver and gold are mine, and the cattle on the thousand hills." Follow then in that way that merits the acceptance of His way and these shall be thine.

Reading 2667–6
53–Year–Old Male, Merchants' Representative

(Q) Why have I been compelled to go through such misfortune in the past three years?

(A) This, as we find, will entail much of that which the body has preached and practiced. As should be known, and as has oft been given by the body, we live, we move, we have our being in Him, the Giver of all good and perfect gifts. That which is in the material world is as lent us of the Lord. When we are in His way and are then in straits, we know sin lieth at the door. "Be not unequally yoked together with unbelievers" may well be called that period, that set about, the initiation of the body mentally, as it were, into the ministry of that which has been the tenets (if not the practice) of the entity for so long.

Then know that if self is kept in the right way He *will* provide. "The silver and the gold is mine, saith the Lord. He that abideth in me shall not want, neither shall there come that upon him that I will not provide with same the way of escape."

Turn ye closer to that ye have professed, and practiced (in a manner), and ye shall see in yourself, in your associations, the *glorifying* of that thou hast held as the ideal–and hast fallen somewhat short in the applications of same.

Reading 5602–1
53–Year–Old Male, Customer Service Representative

As to the mental body, this is very good. Many changes, many alter-ations, in the manner of thinking, the manner of application of that as tenets or ideals of the body. These have been altered and changed in the activities of the body. Some of these have been for good. Some of these have been for consternation, or worriments for the body. These should be that with the ideals, *make* that such as will ever be that which *lifts* up, *looks* up, *sought* for, but ever *beyond* the grasp wholly. Being content with that had in hand; *not* satisfied, not wholly for selfish grati-fications, but not for that of aggrandizement of selfish interests; but in keeping with that as has been held–especially in youth BY the body–as its ideals. Ready for questions.

(*Q*) *Any advice regarding business or financial activities and conditions?*

(A) As is given, the body's mental abilities are efficient–and suffi-cient–in this direction, are the *ideals* and the innate *policies of* the body adhered to. The *consternation*, or changes that have been wrought in the financial situations, financial relations, have been–as the body well knows–by the change, or the listening to policies of others. While, do not become so engrossed in self as to lord self's abilities; yet be of sufficient stability in the application of that held within self, as to be able to handle or carry same through. *These* will be in keeping with that to which the body physically, the body mentally, the body spiritually, may attain. Attaining or using that in hand, one becomes able, capable, efficient in using that as may be *lent*; for that of *earthly* goods is *lended* to an individual to apply in the service of that *whatsoever* a body may worship.

Reading 5475–7
50–Year–Old Male

(*Q*) *How can the body go about to create the harmony that is desired in the home life?*

(A) By taking a stand for that as is known in self as to be the proper, the correct relationships as must and will exist, and keep to that as is known and felt, *irrespective* of *anything* else.

(*Q*) *What Prayer can be held by the body as a guide to that he wishes to attain?*

(A) May the meditations of my heart, of my mind, of my body, be wholly acceptable in thy sight, my Lord and my Redeemer.

(Q) *Considering all physical conditions, what occupation would it be best for the body to take up on returning home?*

(A) This should not be considered too fast, for the inclination will be to worry over same. Will that as has just been given be held, the place, the position, will be seeking the man as much as the man seeking the place.

(Q) *Through whom could the proper connections be made to do this?*

(A) Through any of those that are in a position to use men. Go to Morris Rome!

(Q) *How can the body build courage from within to meet all situations?*

(A) Trust in Him, not in self–and don't be afraid of the other fellow, or what they'll do! So live, so act, as to be able to meet that that is said, thought, or done, in ANY of situations that may come about.

Reading 1257–1
48–Year–Old Female, Widow

Thus doth the soul come to know its awareness. And in the experience with its fellow man draws as it were itself out as to whether it has become worthy of that glory to be in the presence of divinity itself.

For man remains in the presence of same, ever; for His presence abideth. He is nearer than thy hand, than thy mind, if ye will but take hold upon Him...

Know that the *living* forces of thy God are *active!* Not as of stone or wood but as the spirit of truth that casteth out fear, that bringeth peace, that bringeth harmony, that bringeth those things that make for the associations with thy fellow man as a better neighbor, a better sister, a better daughter, a better mother, a better citizen.

These be those things that make for the opening of those awarenesses within that bring the peace that passeth understanding.

In those astrological forces we find one that tends rather to headstrongness, yet with those inclinations to listen but to do one's own way after all. These be not as faults but do not mislead self or those that would aid thee in such an attitude.

Hold fast to that which is *good*, and *seek*; for the seeker shall find. And he that knocketh, to him it shall be opened. And *know* thy Redeemer liveth and hath made intercessions for thee that ye, too, may know the way of life.

In the Venus forces or influences, a sympathetic, a complementary tendency in the activities of the individual, yet the so oft seeking and becoming discouraged because of material things that fade away. Lay not up treasures then in the material things, for these change; but rather in those that are of the spiritual nature, for these bring their reward in themselves. And let the material things, the material possessions, the material blessings, the material surroundings, be as a result rather than an end; let them be as an effect of seeking the Lord while He may be found. For all material things are only lent to be as opportunities for the individual, and that ye have given ye possess. If ye love, ye have given same. If ye would have friends, be friendly. If ye would have joy, make joy in the experience of others. If ye would have crosses to bear, if ye would have harsh words said to thee, if ye would have hard feelings from about, then do such to others and they come of themselves. For that ye sow, that ye must reap.

Reading 4742–1
Adult Female

(Q) Where is my financial support coming from?

(A) Trust in those forces as *have* provided same heretofore, not in thine own self. Know that those things as come through the various activities will be so as to meet that as is necessary for the carrying on.

(Q) What kind of work should I do, and where will I find it?

(A) The outline as given as that which would be well for the body, would be well for the body to consider all the way through. This, as we would find, would come under those of social service, or in those activities as make for the care of individuals as companions with or for individuals, or in some channel of work in that nature. The body would make an excellent companion for someone travelling.

(Q) Where and with whom will I make my home?

(A) Find the body that needs you, and you need them! This may be done through those regular channels where one adapts themselves for such activities.

Reading 1219–1
40–Year–Old Female, Stenographer

And if these experiences are made for self-indulgence, self-aggrandizement first, then there are set up in the experience of the soul false gods.

In making then those applications of self, let the experience be in keeping with that which is not merely idealistic, but having an ideal in the spiritual life so pattern the activities in the material influences that they may be one and the same. And the material effects then may be the result OF the spiritual application. And *not* the material the goal, but as the result of soul development.

Coming in this experience in those environs of April is not the result of the entity's activities in this material plane. It is rather then the indication to the entity, as signs, as omens of what *have* been the experiences of the entity through its sojourns in the earth and what during those activities the entity did *about*, did with, the opportunities for manifesting itself in such a way and manner as to be a channel, a glorifying, an example of Creative Forces through that experience the entity has had.

Reading 4159–3
Adult Male

(Q) *Should the body take out added insurance on his health?*
(A) If he so desires!

(Q) *What writing could the body do that would make a name for him and money too?*
(A) Service, and how one may apply self–and in same may the body assist self in *finding* self.

(Q) *What other means can the body have to improve his financial status?*
(A) Not so much financial, as that as would be given unto the Creator and Maker of all; for when these are supplied in the fullness of self, He if faithful to give those that as is needed in the exultation in *every* way and manner. Be content first with that in hand; not *satisfied*, but studying first to show self approved unto Him, the Giver of all good and perfect gifts. When that is accomplished, He has promised– and His promises are true! Does the body believe? Then *act* that way!

Reading 5563–1
Adult Female

(Q) Inasmuch as it has taken longer to cure her daughter [5562] than was at first anticipated, advise the body how she and her husband can take care of this matter financially.

(A) Prepare self in the manner outlined, placing self in the hands of those forces–call them circumstances, call them what one will or may, it is the power of God–His is the All Force. Believest thou that thou livest in the midst of the Father? Then act that way. Never has there been seen one that wholly trusted in God at want, nor their seed begging bread.

Reading 2398–2
42-Year-Old Male, Portrait Artist

There are the abilities in those fields of art, those fields of service of various natures and characters; that bring the temperamental problems when interpreted in material things.

Then, let the entity first know:

Do not disturb self as respecting the material things. If thy purpose is kept aright, these will be brought into those lines of activity as to supply the needs of the physical man.

Not that this assurance gives thee the privilege of being a spendthrift, to satisfy only material desires. For, the entity must keep self in those manners in which there is the desire to give honest, sincere service in thy activities; that the glory of Him may be manifested, who hast endowed thee with such abilities–yea, who has commissioned thee in thy ways of preserving for mankind the beauties of the Law of laws in man's experience. For, these are only heaven sent.

Keep thy mind, thy body, in accord with these, and ye will find beauty in all thy relationships.

Ready for questions.

(Q) In my work, should I stress portraits, types, or landscapes and scenes?

(A) These should be varied. There should be certain portions of time given to landscapes, for that portion of the public to which this appeals; and there will be found greater outlet for same in some communities or centers. However, portraits are those that will bring the most satisfactory remuneration or physical or monetary returns. Studies are well, but not these so much as the others.

Reading 1538–1
41-Year-Old Male, Food Products Manager

(Q) *Direct me to work which will enable me to support my family and which will also be that I am fitted for.*

(A) These may be only–must be–accomplished within self. What is thy purpose? Set thine own house in order within thine self *First!* Then, these may be brought about.

The *results* are those activities that are the creative influence within the mental self towards its ideal. And the results may be that as the outcome, *not* that as set as the first and foremost, see?

(Q) *Should I seek for employment in Norfolk or outside of Norfolk?*

(A) Wherever there may be those very channels or characters as may be indicated.

As we find, around Quantico would be the better; or Yorktown, or the like.

(Q) *How may I fit myself better for this work?*

(A) That's what we have been trying to tell you all the time! If you can't see it, it's too bad!

Reading 2369–1
43-Year-Old Female

(Q) *If necessary to move, in what part of the city would it be best for me to go?*

(A) That must be chosen by self.

(Q) *What should be my life's work?*

(A) This may be more apparent from the combinations of the life's activities, than from a physical approach; but as we find, that in which there is a *semblance* or direct activity in *supplying* helpful influences in the lives or associations of others. Then, either as a teacher or as a minister to those individuals less fortunate than self, or in making for entertainments for others, or as an inn keeper or the like.

(Q) *How may I best be able to meet my obligations financially?*

(A) These must be applied first spiritually, mentally, and the right thinking, if there will be brought better conditions. These must be within self and not from others.

(Q) Please give me some spiritual advice?

(A) *Know* thy ideal; not what others should do for you, but what you may do for others–physically, mentally, spiritually.

Then, study to show self approved unto that ideal; never condemning others. For, the law is, that if ye would not be condemned, condemn not!

Reading 1487–1
65–Year–Old Female, Writer

(Q) Will my biography of Edwin Markham be taken by publisher?

(A) It should–it will.

(Q) Will my book of poems be taken by publisher?

(A) These will be somewhat later, but these will be taken.

(Q) How may I clear up my financial troubles?

(A) Leaning on Him. For the silver and the gold are the Lord's, and the way that leads to the more perfect understanding is to trust the more wholly in Him.

Let this be as thy meditations, in thine own words but this as the thought:

"Lord, thy servant, thy handmaid, seeks ever to be in accord; yea, in attune with Thee–and Thy purposes Thou hast for me in this experience among the children of men.

"As Thou hast loved, then, and given Thyself a ransom for the many, wilt Thou in Thy love guide and direct in the way as Thou hast promised?

"For my trust is ever in Thee! Lead on, o Lord–lead Thou, O Lord, on!"

Reading 2786–1
45–Year–Old Female

(Q) What suggestion and advice may be given me at this time regarding the advisability of another marriage?

(A) This as we find may come about in a year or two, but remember–as has been given–with the present companion it has not been finished as yet. There *must* be the more perfect understanding, before there is the full release.

(Q) Considering the financial difficulties involved in my present situation, what

steps should I take to insure security for my family and myself?

(A) Study to show thyself approved first unto God. He knoweth what thou hast need of. Do as ye would be done by. This is the greatest assurance. Not that ye do not meet material needs with material conditions. For, rendering unto Caesar the things that are Caesar's and unto God the things that are God's, is a part of the material law, the material experience. But these will be assurances, if thy purpose, if thy desire, if thy hope is in the things of the Lord.

(Q) *What have been the past associations with my son [...] and when will I see him again in this experience?*

(A) As we find, the closer association with [...] was in the Egyptian land, when He was called or sent away–and then came again. He will come again into thine experience here.

Reading 1472–6
58–Year–Old Female, Writer, Radio Broadcaster

(Q) *Will I ever have sufficient financial freedom to enable me to work without consideration of money, and if so when?*

(A) This of course–as to every one *minded* of material welfare–presents a problem.

When self is turned entirely loose, and the reliance is upon Him … How did He give? Consider the lilies of the valley. They toil not, neither do they spin; yet Solomon in all his glory was not arrayed as one of these!

When taking thought of the morrow, do you add one cubit to your stature? do you add one hope? Rather you add one stumbling stone or a stepping-stone.

Consider, as He gave, the birds of the air they are His and He provideth for them. Did He not give you these? Do you hold to the world and to spiritual truths also? Or do you apply them in thy hopes, in thy problems, in thy activities?

Yea, ye call this impractical–for ye are in a practical and a commercial and a business world, and these must be considerations. Yea–but how usest thou them?

Yes, it will come to thee if ye apply thyself. Whose *is* the silver and the gold? Whose *is* the power, the might, the light, the hope? Who is the giver of these? They that serve Him. These are lent to those who are His. They are opportunities, then, in thy own experience.

(Q) *Should I withdraw the money I have for investment with the Young Management Corporation, or leave it there?*

(A) For the present, leave it there. After October, remove it . . .

(Q) *What work can I do to lessen the crimes and injustices against the children of the world?*

(A) Whose children are they?

These problems are only—ye may sow the seed day by day and leave the results of their growth to Him that doeth all things well. Great is the inclination in many—and it groweth in thee—"I would see that I would do come to full *power* in the moment!"

The knowledge of God, the correction of things and conditions, is a growth.

He then that would be the greater must be content—not satisfied, but content—in doing today; wherever it may be spoken, wherever it may be written *against* such—not as Ye deem a crime, but that which is against the tenets of His "Suffer little children to come unto me, for of such is the kingdom of God."

Only in that attitude and that approach. He careth for them.

All of thy boasting, all of thy ranting or raving may not change one. It is only what ye do with those ye meet day by day.

As ye speak to those even that are *considered* not capable of thinking, ye may do so in such a manner that the crimes against the young in every walk and phase may take root and grow to be miracles or crimes!

That ye have become cognizant of it shows that ye must do something about it! Not that ye may make laws, not that ye may control laws; but ye can *live* that ye believe!

(Q) *Before my spiritual awakening I had ample opportunity to use my writing ability. Since I have been thus enlightened the utilization of this gift has seemed blocked in every direction. Why is this and what can I do to regain that opportunity?*

(A) Whom He loveth He chasteneth, and He purgeth every one—that they may bring forth *more* fruit, *better* fruit!

Or how did He give? The children of this world *appear* to be wiser, in their *own* generation, than the children of light.

Are ye not able, are ye not willing to drink of the cup of which ye have taken hold…?

(Q) *Have you any further instructions or suggestions you would care to give me for my work and service?*

(A) We would care to give you all! Will ye take hold of that ye have today?

Then turn within and take thyself to task. Not as to whether ye may eat tomorrow or not, but say to thy soul—not to thy body, "[1472], where leadest thou thy neighbor?"

Reading 262–109
Study Group Reading, Lesson on "Happiness"

And as has been set to song, if you will count your happiness, your blessings day by day, they are many more than that you have even any right to find fault in.

For if the earth is the Lord's, and if your brother is in the image of your Maker, have you any right—ever—to find fault? or to speak un-kindly? much less unjustly?

And what is the first law? Like begets like! For in the act, as in the seed, is the full grown blossom of what you do, what you think, what you are! Hence if you sow Happiness will you reap turmoil? or riot? Rather in the still small voice, do you find the song of Happiness, the blessings of divine love directing, guiding, keeping your ways.

What matter if there is no new dress, hat, shoes, or even the house rent paid? They are of the moment. If you are happy that you are alive, you still have the opportunity to say, "Blessings be on thee," and these are what live forever. Shadows pass. Only the light and truth lives on. Disturbances and distresses pass. For you say "God is in His holy temple, let all the earth keep silent." What do you mean? Is it just a saying because you have heard it oft, or do you really believe it?

Then, as His children, *act that way!*

Reading 1463–1
58-Year-Old Female, Poet

For much might be said, as we have indicated heretofore, for the purposes and desires that *prompt* the entity called [510] in her activity as a service to others.

With the associations, then, let the policies, the purposes, be not alone for the material gain. For remember, these should be ever secondary. While it is true that in a material world the material things are necessities for material activities, if the promptings of the activities are of a *constructive* nature, *God*–or the Creative Force, or the Divine–gives the increase.

For man may not do other than be the channel through which the increase of *any* nature may arise. For God alone gives the increase.

Then, in such an association, with those activities, those purposes as the ideals of the activities, we may bring, we may expect results.

And if you do not expect, how *can* it be creative? For the increase in material things, in the activities that are necessary to be increased to meet that need that would *continue* for the soul development?

For the purposes of each entity, each soul, in a manifested experience, should ever be to do whatever is necessary for the full awakening of the purpose that the Creative Force or God, or the Universal Energy (or whatever term may be necessary for the individual awakening) might be expressed.

For only with the purpose held in that direction may there be the vision of the glory that is prepared for those that seek to know His Face.

Use the abilities, then, in the direction that has been awakened so oft; that alone has kept the *efforts of the entity* as a *growing* experience. For know that only as we sow do we reap.

As you then sow *constructive* influences into the lives and experiences of others, you make such growth in your *own* relationships to the Whole.

(Q) What is the next step in my work and career?

(A) This has just been indicated. Be sincere with self as to your purposes and desires, knowing that you must, that you will, that you do make them constructive in the experiences of others to *know* hope and faith and charity.

(Q) What suggestions can you make as to how to proceed, now, in business and professional ways, so that my Product, in Books, Recitals, Creative Writings, shall bring adequate returns?

(A) Just as has been indicated. These are that as should be the basis of every entity's activity in a material experience. And these are they; being true to self and to the voice within. For know, He has promised to meet thee in the tabernacle of thine *own* individual self! In that manner, then–as you turn within. And as has been said of old, being true then to that self thou wilt not be false to any.

Build truth, honesty, integrity; and patience.

For as Time and Space and Patience in a three-dimensional world are *as* manifestations of Truth into the experiences of souls of men, so impressing upon the minds to use these in expressions of faith and hope and love there may be brought the constructive forces of every nature.

For the silver and gold are the Lord's, and ye would *not* then cheat thine own soul by the use or misuse of that of any nature that would be a manifestation of the Love Divine that maketh the world anew day by day.

Reading 257–34
35–Year–Old Sales Manager

There has been some change in the physical, mental and spiritual development of the body. These are, in the general, for the good. There are many conditions that are worrying, aggravating, fretting the body; yet these, would the body follow in that way as has been persistently given that the body should look toward self's application and the remuneration will be forthcoming–while true these seem to be unsatisfactory, and there seems that there is not the proper cooperation or understanding that there should be–viewed alone from the materialistic, or viewed alone from the individual standpoint, this may or may not be true–but viewed from the larger sense, the conditions will be made satisfactory.

Do not lose the temper and say things that the body will, or would, be sorry for. Rather consider what would be said to self were the conditions reversed. This, possibly the body would say at first hand, could not exist with positions reversed! yet, were the body to take stock of self, innately there will be seen that oft times have there been conditions when there was not so much in *action physically* in the same direction, but thought, intent, and the *desire* was put in motion, and the body reaping the fruits of that force, power, let loose in–would you say unguarded moment? No, but rather in the training, in the making, of one capable, with the abilities to handle not only small things but large things, large deals, large *individuals* in mental capacity! large undertakings as an executive. While this not the policy wholly, but the body was just a bit too *premature* in some of the things expressed to its associates–*not* superiors, no! *Associates*, yet in the capacity of superiors, when it comes to the *financial* end of the proposition.

Reading 257–78
38-Year-Old Sales Manager

(Q) *How can I now reach the material success in 1932 to be able to better carry out my ideals?*

(A) So act that thine ideals are in accord with HIS will. Let the success, let the bounty or the little, be in HIS hands. THAT the better way.

Reading 257–244
49-Year-Old Male, Sales Manager

In connection with making a success, and of individual associations in various departments–and in connection with individuals handling various branches or phases of associations–success depends upon what is termed success. For, man may gain the whole world and lose his own soul, as many are doing under the existent circumstances.

Rather, in this direction, counsel would be according to that given of old: *Today there is set before thee good and evil, life and death.* There are the opportunities in the present for individuals so associated or connected, as self, to disregard their fellow men and consider self and the accumulating of material things.

The material world passeth away, for this endureth not–and many through these trying periods and experiences will find, as ye in thy associations are finding, that individuals of wealth and position, yea well-thought of by their associates, are experiencing that their hearts and minds are dark with fear and doubt. Yet they are driven on and *on* to consider only the might and power; some by their social position, some by their connections in political and financial circles. Yea, they are successes, materially–yet how much of such a success can they present before a merciful God?

Then, in thy considering–thou knowest the way, physically, mentally and spiritually. Let that be the guide, for the law of the Lord is perfect.

As to individuals–that should be according to *whatever* is thy choice, as in connection with those that may assist in carrying out plans. Instill in those, also, the *ideal* of success.

These should be first–do the first things first!

As to the associations and connections in various war departments–these, too, remember, are men–as thyself; some with ideals of questionable nature, some with the desire to be ahead in one direction or another. And yet a word here or there will oft keep that correct balance.

Never attempt *anything* to get ahead of another, nor do or be ruled by spite or hate. This in *all* of thy connections will bring a good conscience.

Never do that which will be questioned in thine own mind as to whether it is merely good business, merely "scotching," merely feathering the nest. But rather, "What will the Lord have me do?"

In that attitude there needs never be fear of there not being, through these periods, sufficient–and more than sufficient–to carry on.

Ready for questions.

(Q) *Is it better for me to dispose of all common stocks and keep the money in cash or government bonds?*

(A) In government bonds, as we find, would be the better–or the greater portion. Sufficient cash to meet the various needs, to be sure, but keep the full quota of bonds.

(Q) *What is the best situation for a person who doesn't want to gamble but who wants to conservatively retain what he has?*

(A) This, under the present circumstances and conditions, is to invest in real estate *and* in bonds. If there is a correct understanding, this is the natural or nature's way of improving the status in such conditions.

Reading 459–12
44–Year–Old Female, Widow

As the law has been and is a portion of the hopes–as the associations are still many of the problems of the moment–find the solution in the choices as in keeping with these:

Thou hast seen the way of the Lord. Thou knowest it to be good. Depart not from same for the satisfying or the gratifying of material wishes or material desires. For, the law of the Lord is perfect; and they that seek to follow in His way shall not find themselves among those disturbed, nor among the children of want.

Reading 2489-1
48-Year-Old Male, Field Supervisor

(Q) *Would it be well to consider the real estate business?*

(A) Not as satisfactory. Though this is in line, of course, with that field indicated, we find it is not as satisfactory as would be an association with banks or the like, or an association for the distribution of manufactured goods.

(Q) *Should I consider the bulb business with Mr. Pierce of Orlando, Fla.*

(A) This is again bordering on the type of activity indicated, but this is not the best. It may be used, to be sure, as a stepping-stone for the next. But know what you want, and then go after it!

(Q) *Would this enable me to meet my increasing financial obligations during the next few years, especially to educate my daughters?*

(A) As we find, if there is the application of self, have no fear that there will not be the provisions made–through the activities of self and its associations and connections–for the carrying on of duties, as well as the privileges of such an education or activity.

Keep in those directions that are set before thee. These directions for the activities will bring about the associations and connections that bring the best influence in the experience of the entity.

Reading 520-2
31-Year-Old Male

While material successes in the entity's experience have been more or less of the spasmodic nature, these may be expected until the entity has so set self in a manner in which the *soul* development, the *mental* development, is put above those of material gains. True, in a material world material conditions are which individuals or others judge an individual's success; yet the contentment that lies from within from a life spent in a service for others–wherein the physical, the mental, the spiritual are treated as a unit, and that all forces work together for good when these are aligned in those of the soul's development–these, to the entity, have been principles in the whole of the entity's experience, while there have been periods when the entity has gone to excess in first one way then another. Now, there is today set before thee good and evil. Choose that which would be well spoken of by others for the physical gains, or that which will bring content, peace that passeth understanding from within, in that hope that may be builded in the lives of individuals through the efforts of the entity in those directions that bring for the better things.

Ready for questions.

(Q) What is his rightful vocation?

(A) Peoples, rather than things.

(Q) Should he continue his present activities?

(A) A change–a time–has come. Would be well in the change, that the individual, the entity, consider well those channels, those conditions surrounding those forces through which the entity is gaining, is seeing self in the present. These are worthy of acceptation. Are they compatible to thine own understanding, then work for it!

(Q) Should he become associated with the Green Mountains Camps?

(A) That would be decided within self. The other may present itself beforehand. Then, consider well–and choose as self would see. Not that as will bring for just the money, but that that will bring into the lives of individuals that which may help physically, mentally, the soul, the development of many.

(Q) Would his association be successful both to the camps and to his personal and business welfare?

(A) If so chosen, it can be made so.

(Q) What will be the future of the Green Mountains Adult Camps, as well as the children's camps?

(A) That depends upon the manner in which the administration of same is conducted. As to give the future of anything, that dependent upon the thought–and *active* thought–of individuals; for, as was given of old, "Be thou fruitful and multiply; subdue the earth and that therein". It didn't say abuse the earth or that therein, nor use for thine own aggrandizement; for only that that may be personally used from day to day is necessary. Considerest thou the lily and its beauty? It toils not, neither does it spin; yet Solomon in all his glory not arrayed as one of these. Wilt thou, then, thine self, be a channel? or wilt thou attempt to turn the channels into thine own doing?

(Q) *Who would be of most help to him in accomplishing his life's work?*

(A) Himself, and that from within–and finding the ideal to which the entity may hope to point another, in assisting self to attain same.

(Q) *What can be done to improve his standing in his daily activities?*

(A) Act like a man of God, as a son of the Most High, and keep self in a position to answer for the thoughts that come from within, avoiding those things that so easily beset human desires; rather hitch thine aspirations, thine desires, to be *one with* the *holy* things of life.

(Q) *Why hasn't he been as successful as he would like to have been?*

(A) Indecisions from within self.

(Q) *How can he improve his business ability? Give constructive comment.*

(A) Study to show thyself approved unto God. Be not ashamed of labors lowly or high. Seek not to find the favor in the eyes of people. Rather *choose* to *know* thou hast favor with God, for the silver and the gold is His. Forsake not that as was given to him, [Solomon?] in the desires of thine heart thou mayest know the way to those successes that be of the worldly nature, and of the mental and spiritual nature. In gaining an understanding–and, in *all* thine getting, *get* understanding. In attaining same, those things that make *for* fame, fortune, success– these are a *natural* expectant result; when used, *not* abused.

(Q) *Would you recommend him to marry before the time stated in a previous reading?*

(A) That's with him! It has been given as that which is best. First find self.

(Q) *Where should he establish his permanent home?*

(A) Close to whatever portion, or whatever part of the work itself that the entity undertakes. Consider those sources or channels as given, through which the information is given–now–and the needs of same.

(Q) *How can he best serve his immediate family?*

(A) By serving self; not as self-i-s-h-l-y, but he that is true to *self* will not be false to family!

(Q) How can he best serve mankind?
(A) In service to mankind, is first gaining the understanding, the knowledge of self, the needs–and little by little; not *big* things–for these are the outgrowth of the small things; for acorns are not timbers, neither is the electron the large dynamo; neither is the stone the center of the building–yet these added to, grown in grace, in knowledge, in understanding, become the basis for *all* things.

Reading 520–4
35–Year–Old Male, Follow–Up Reading

There may be seen about the entity in its associations with individuals or groups that which is as of a seeking, as an unrest upon the part of many who are not stable in their higher mental and spiritual selves, who are seeking for that not only by which they may prepare their lives, as they express themselves now, but that they may rely upon in their meditation, in their depressed or in their exalted moments. That which has been and is the motivative influence that arises from the individual or an individual making an ideal that may be gained only in its realm of experience but which may be sought for as expressing itself in the material things in life as it makes for its associations with man. For, as this:

The love of life, or the continuity of love, of life, as expresses itself in a creative force or God, that shows its manifestations in the manner in which such an individual treats his fellow man, is such that makes for the advancement, the stabilizing of individuals. And such data, such expressions, such matter may the entity in *its* seeking and its expression give to many. For as has been seen in those experiences of the entity, the soul, in the earth as it expresses itself in matter or in form under or during varied experiences, there has been that gathering of data that made for the showing or the expressing of the disposition of this or that group as related to other groups in their varied activities or associations. So the entity in the present may make these for the ideal; not idealistic without a practical application. For, as is expressed, the love of God as it expresses itself in the manner of mien of an individual towards his fellow man is only a practical thing.

So does the earth and its associated activities advance. So does that called civilization; so that called brotherly love. And, as given of old, it is not as to who will ascend into the heaven to bring him down, or who will go over the sea that we might know His face or name, but "Lo, ye will find Him in thine own heart." In thine own mind and thine own expression to thy fellow man, in doing as has been given; "As ye would that men should do to you, do ye even so to them."

(Q) *How can I prevent the entanglements in the business in Providence from curtailing my activities in the directions mentioned above?*

(A) It is not by some great deed that the greater accomplishments are made, but a word here, an expression there; and it's line upon line, precept upon precept. These take not from, but as He has promised: Use that opportunity thou hast in hand day by day. As ye use same, as ye give out, the next step, the next opportunity is given. For man may sow, man may speak, *man* may make manifest those laws, those expressions of an All–Wise Creator from the abundance of his heart, but only the Father, God, may give the increase. Doth man attempt to set himself in the position of demanding this or that, it is *self*–exaltation rather than being just a channel through which the glory of the Father in his love for the fellow man may be made manifest.

Then, it will *not*–it *does* not–interfere; only in so far as there is builded within the own consciousness that there are not the opportunities for the study or for the expression that is desired *of self*. But use rather this:

"As my opportunity comes, let me be the channel for the expression of, the glory of, that in my own life and that towards my fellow man."

(Q) *Will you please give an example or illustration of the kind or type of data referred to, on which I should work?*

(A) As the observations are made from day to day of this or that that disturbs the associate or the friend, or the foe, whom the entity may contact, there will be seen that–as this is put down in, we might say, black and white–these may be correlated as from one to another, see? Then the experience of self in how that the less and less of self and the more and more of the ideal is held within the experience of such an one, the more and more does the growth or the help or the understanding come. And the entity in its contact may give a word here or there. And trouble not thyself that some may rebuke thee, or some may even find fault; but know within thyself thou art doing what thine heart, thine ideal, thine relationship with thy creative force, thy God, would have thee do. And He, in His own time, brings the result in thine *own* experience and in that of thy brother that thou wouldst aid.

Today thou hast seen in thine experience this that has disturbed one as respecting his own physical and material and mental associations. Thou may speak to such an one, and make note of that which has prevented such from accepting or opening self for a greater under-standing. And then in the next thou mayest find that in such do ye grow; not as by leaps and bounds, for in the acorn or in the grain of wheat may be enfolded the whole of first the shoot, the stalk, the flower, then the whole that is a growth. So are the words of truth, if they are prompted by or from thine inner self toward thy fellow man; not for self but that the glory of the Father through thee may find its expres-sion and growth in material world. For matter is the expression of spirit *moving* in the material world. The mind is the builder in which there are all of its phases and manifestations. And thou hast set before thee a *great* undertaking. Be thou faithful to that which has been entrusted unto thee. From whom? From the Creative Forces that find manifesta-tion in thine inner self.

Reading 3051–4
45–Year–Old Female

(Q) What lesson for either of us to learn so not to bring condition back into another experience?

(A) This should come with [3436] not for [3051].

(Q) What can [3051] do to overcome her husband's lack of generosity to her financially?

(A) Let [3051] be just as generous to the husband as she expects the husband to be to her, and these will be more in accord and will bring greater harmony in the relationships throughout the experience. These each have ideals. Make them coordinate with the material, the mental and the spiritual lives of each. Know that it must begin in the spiritual. Then material results will be brought into the experience as the mind is controlled towards those ideals set by each as to the spirit with which they will control and act in relationships one to another.

(Q) To what extent will inflation affect [3436]'s business, advise if wise to change

to another business, if so what business?

(A) As indicated, insurance and real estate.

(Q) How successful would the land investment in Staten Island–[3436] has in mind be?

(A) Not a very successful venture. There are too many disturbances soon to arise, especially relating to some of the holdings.

(Q) Which pieces of property would be the best investment for such a project?

(A) Wherever he would choose for his activities. Do not have these in one area and the activities of self in another.

Reading 303–6
48–Year–Old Female, Bookkeeper

There will come those strengthening influences in the material, there will come the change in the desires, in the activities of those about thee to make for greater blessings.

And as ye hold to that which ye have purposed in thine heart to do, then leave the rest with him and fear not to trust; and be not unmindful or doubtful that those things that are of the material-material are His also. For "The silver and the gold is mine, saith the Lord. I will repay to those that are faithful unto the end." The darker shadows are just before the dawn. Hold to that thou hast in thine experience, and ye shall find harmony and peace and understanding coming in all the associations, both those in the material relationships and those in the life in the home, and in the relationships to others; all will find in the experiences and expressions of same that which will make thee cry the more and the more, "Blessed is the name of the Lord!"

Ready for questions.

(Q) What are the first steps I should take to meet my pressing financial difficulties?

(A) As we find, there are channels that are even almost unknown to the body that are being opened up in this direction. But in those relationships about the home, and those surroundings and those things there, these–as we find–through those regular channels that have been opened and are opening for the body–may be met in the ways that will be shown thee...

(Q) Any spiritual advice that will help me personally at this time?

(A) Study to show thyself approved in that manner that thine own conscience does not smite thee.

(Q) *Is there a possibility that we may learn to use the law that Jesus used in controlling those things material and spiritual to meet present needs?*

(A) This can be in the experience of all.

Reading 1219–1
40–Year–Old Female, Stenographer

But if there is the ideal, in whatever phase of endeavor, that given is to bring a little cleaner life, a little more of hope, a little more of cheer, a thinking more of creative influences and forces–*then* the entity may find the experiences not only productive of that which brings within the mental self greater harmony, but the opportunities for the material gain will also be enhanced.

Reading 2087–3
Given for Atlantic University

In the administering of ideals, in the planning of policies, the great care should be had in that these are in keeping with those tenets as will make it possible for those forces, those vibrations, those elements of understanding and inner consciousness, to be made manifest to those that *minister* and serve in the various capacities as ministers, or servants of mankind, in and through this channel. This done, the character, the characteristics of each that minister in their various phase of ministration, should be well–grounded in that understanding that their portion, their phase of ministry, is but a manifestation of the whole in its particular sphere of ministry. This done, little fear may be had respecting resources, or those of *material* things necessary to carry on. Remembering that as of old, they labored one with another–for they all had a mind to work for the building up of an house to establish His name there. Then, let thine yeas be yea–thy nays be nay, but little by little, line upon line, *minister*–even as it is given thee. Not in exaltation of self in *any* of those phases of desire as respecting the selfish exaltation, but rather in humbleness of spirit, serving the weaker, that the *strength of* the Lord be made *manifest* in and through those offices.

Each should, then, be made aware that they are but channels

through which each trustee, each minister, each teacher, each inter-preter, may assist those who present themselves for the study, that they may *glorify* Him, and there will be added unto the number such as are called; for those whom He called did He predestine–that they might through *such* offices be given the *opportunity* to make manifest the expe-riences as are given them.

Ready for questions.

(Q) *Would it be well, then, that each professor be interviewed and be presented with some of the ideal?*

(A) There should not be chosen even the *messenger* or the janitor, nor the president, without instilling that those are the *ideals…*

(Q) *What part should each of us play, or are we fitted to play, in the ministration?*

(A) Ministering as to the policies that *must be* followed by the faculty in *its* administering to the needs of those pupils that seek through this channel for the understanding of what life is all about; making life not only good, but good for something.

4

●

Being of Service and Putting to Use What You Already Possess

Reading 2067–1
52–Year–Old Female, Teacher

The natural inclinations and tendencies of the entity, as will be seen, particularly from the material sojourns, influence or urge the entity to become and be a seeker.

This one principle the entity must gain, or become more aware of—if the greater understanding, the greater knowledge would be attained, or the greater good accomplished:

It is in the giving of that which is attained that the abilities come for greater comprehension and understanding.

This applies not only in the material. For, in this present day—though hardships make it necessary for the consideration of economic influences, and many activities have caused the entity to oft curtail its efforts in some directions—fame and fortune will be the lot of the entity in this experience, unless there is a failing entirely in the use of that which *is* in hand.

In considering the interpretation of the records here—this as we find may be said to be a composite of not only the material sojourns, but of the sojourns in the interims between the material sojourns.

And these (the material sojourns) have been many. Thus there has been confusion of many natures in this present experience. Gradually, though, the entity has grown to comprehend—not so much because of necessity as because of the earnest seeking and the desire to be used as a channel through which hope, help, aid, might come to others.

This is the greater influence for good in the experience of this entity, and it is that which is to be cultivated the more throughout this experience; *yet* in somewhat more of an humble manner than the mien has indicated at times.

For, as has been suggested, these are the composites:

Oft the entity is considered by others to be too sure of itself without sufficient proof of the source of the knowledge as may be presented to others.

Hence the interest in the occult, and the interest in spiritual things.

Reading 2807–3
36–Year–Old Female

In the administering of ideals, in the planning of policies, the great care should be had in that these are in keeping with those tenets as will make it possible for those forces, those vibrations, those elements of understanding and inner consciousness, to be made manifest to those that *minister* and serve in the various capacities as ministers, or servants of mankind, in and through this channel. This done, the character, the characteristics of each that minister in their various phase of ministration, should be well-grounded in that understanding that their portion, their phase of ministry, is but a manifestation of the whole in its particular sphere of ministry. This done, little fear may be had respecting resources, or those of *material* things necessary to carry on. Remembering that as of old, they labored one with another—for they all had a mind to work for the building up of an house to establish His name there. Then, let thine yeas be yea—thy nays be nay, but little by little, line upon line, *minister*—even as it is given thee. Not in exaltation of self in *any* of those phases of desire as respecting the selfish exaltation, but rather in humbleness of spirit, serving the weaker, that the *strength of* the Lord be made *manifest* in and through those offices.

Reading 1404–1
55–Year–Old Female, "Psychosynthesist"

(Q) *Just what particular phase of my work should be stressed in order that I may have greater success with my patients?*

(A) As has just been indicated. Analyses and how they are applied.

(Q) *Just how can I carry on my work so as to bring financial security?*

(A) In the ways as has been indicated; for that ye give, that ye have. And as you give more and more He that is the life, the hope of the world, the fruits will come. For the silver and the gold, and the cattle upon a thousand hills are His. As ye in thy service then merit the use, the lending of these to thy activities, ye have thy assurance of material security. Rather grow more and more in that attitude of "Lord, here am I—use me as thou seest fit. Thou knowest the cares, Thou knowest the things that make afraid. Cleanse me, that I may be the greater channel of blessings to others in this experience. Supply Thou the hand; as Thou didst feed the thousands, so keep me, O God, in the right ways!"

Grow in that, depend upon that; for all of these are *only* the true way.

Reading 2136–1
25–Year–Old Female, Teacher

Taking, then, all those influences—as that to which the entity may build in the present:

Use that thou hast in hand today; for, as the opportunity, as the time comes for the giving out, be sure it is ever seasoned well with the words of truth that make for developments in the experiences of others to-wards constructive influences leading to God—for he that abides in Him shall want for nothing.

Reading 1319–2
56–Year–Old Female, Widow

(Q) *Is the property being managed right?*

(A) As has been indicated portions of same, where there is very good cooperation, are very well. Those where there is lack of this, these we would dispose of.

(Q) *What advice can you give me to doing something to earn money, as I have four families depending on my support? I worry and can't sleep over it.*

(A) As we would find, from those activities where there have been the incomes, the helps and the aids that have been given for others, from those characters and natures may there be expected to come resources to carry on.

For that ye give of yourself in service to others, that ye retain. These come back to self—as in the sowing of good deeds. These are not as idle words but if the service is given that ye may have good things only, you already have your reward. But in keeping in the helpfulness for others, in the activities in that direction may there come the greater service to self, to those dependent upon self.

And ye know in whom ye have put thy trust; ye should know—ye do know. Ye have only lost thy hold, thy grip, by the things and for the things that are of the moment.

For the earth is the Lord's. Trust rather in Him. And as ye do to others may it be done to thee.

Reading 1397–2
58–Year–Old Female, Chiropractor and Naturopath

(Q) *My desire is to have sufficient leisure and release from strain to pursue my study and contact with the "rays" which are operating through the various machines now in use—such as radionics, micro-dynameter, aetheronics and others of a similar nature. In order to accomplish this a certain amount of economic security is necessary.* May I expect this to come through my Texas property? *If so, how soon?*

(A) This should rather be, "Lord, is this the channel, is this the manner in which thou would have me serve? If so, then may those channels, in the activities in the Texas lands, be such that there may be provided that security for my giving of myself in the best of my mind and my body to serve in such a way and manner," and *leave* the results with Him!

These may not be at first, to thee, very definite. But it is *His* way that He would have with thee, if ye would come to know, if ye would be of the greater service in this material experience.

Then, as ye fit thyself in *sincere* desire, so may those channels *furnish* the material things for the carrying out of that He has purposed for thee.

And as ye do they will, they *will* supply that needed.

(Q) *In connection with the Texas property, am I to expect further interference and disloyalty in the future or more cooperation from [...] my former associate, who is now occupying the property?*

(A) As we find, as that ye mete out, if ye expect—if ye show greater cooperation, then ye will find greater cooperation. And remember, the silver and the gold, yea the cattle in the hills, yea the oil, the gold of same, are the Lord's.

Use then that thou hast in hand. For He will multiply it, some to ten, some to twenty, to some sixty, to some an hundred fold; dependent upon that purpose and that sincerity to which thou, thyself, may use that in hand.

Ye may expect, ye may *command*, greater cooperation and greater activity for the fulfilling of same, if thy purposes are set. Not in fame for self, not in fortune for self, but rather that through the channels, through those activities that are permitted in thy hands, in thy keeping, ye may serve thy fellow man the better; bringing to men's consciousness the awareness of their needs, not only mentally but spiritually.

And these will bring thee, then, to thy goal.

Reading 2087–4
Given for Atlantic University

Gertrude Cayce: You will have before you Atlantic University, the President and Trustees of same, and especially certain prospective members of the faculty of this institution. You will give information concerning the best method of selecting the members of the faculty and will answer such questions as you will be asked concerning certain individuals who are now under consideration as possible instructors in the institution.

Edgar Cayce: Yes. In the selection of individuals to act in the capacity of the institution with the tentative policies as are *to* be instituted in same, would be *well* that the President—or those *choosing* such ones—interview personally those that are to be considered, and their qualifications as related to the conduct of the classes or that portion of the whole as is to be conducted by that individual, and *see* that there is at least the tentative cooperation of the said individual *with* those policies, *with* those conditions as has been given as necessary *for* each to be in a position to fill such a place; knowing that each must be well-grounded in the fact that it is service to be *rendered* first and foremost, before consideration of the wherewithal or the *monetary* conditions, see? And, as has been suggested, none should be *qualified* until they know, from President *and* some of the Trustees—or the Trustees as a body—*of* that policy.

Reading 254–5
Given on the Cayce Work

(Q) *As these individuals are depending entirely upon the income received from the readings which are given, and which is not of sufficient amount for their sustenance and the further support of the work, you will give explicit information and suggestions as to how a sufficient amount may be obtained.*

(A) When there is credence given in the heart, mind, soul and body of those depending upon the forces of such manifest conditions, then there is sufficient of the earthly needs supplied through those sources, and "he that having put his hand to the plow and turns back is worse than the infidel." [1 Tim. 5:8]

In the present conditions there needs be a more thorough understanding from and to all those who have already given credence to the benefits that are, have been and may be received through such work, and that the work is depending upon the support of same through the goodness, the consciousness, the ever willing soul, spirit, physical force that will supply those needs necessary to care for those giving of their selves. For the Lord has said, "The gold and silver is mine, and the cattle upon a thousand hills, and he that abideth in me shall ask and receive, and sufficient unto the day [are] the needs thereof. Consider the lilies; how they grow. They toil not, neither do they spin, yet Solomon in all his glory was not arrayed as one of these."

When thou doest the work that guides the creatures of His making more closely to Him, thou only hast to ask and thou will receive. Be not dismayed. Be not afraid, for whatsoever a man soweth that shall he also reap. Be up and doing with a heart that fainteth not, for "I am the way, the truth and the light. No man *cometh unto the* Father but by me, and whatsoever thou asketh in my name, that will the Father give unto thee."

Be not afraid.

Reading 254–17
Given on the Cayce Work

(Q) *The people who gathered at the home of Morton Blumenthal, Tuesday evening at between 9 and 11 o'clock, November 25, 1924, 60 West 68th St., Apartment 102. Are they the right people to help further the work from the standpoint of the physician, the magazine, and the study of problems of phenomena of life?*

(A) These or others. In these we find this same injunction as has been given. Those are the correct ones to assist in the development, in the propagation, of the magazine, in the building of the institute, who have first found the works of such phenomena in their individual lives, and have such phenomena that such revelations as come, that that entity desires to be of assistance to others without the desire of personal aggrandizement of any character first; for we know with any work, and endeavor, "the laborer is worthy of the hire." Yet this must never be placed first and foremost. Without money, position or fame, but the innate desire to serve and to give that others may have the awakening from within. In this particular group, we find the greater number of these interested to that degree, and many who desire to serve. There are many others who will be attracted to such group from time to time, and the work only needs that impetus necessary, that others may know and have the knowledge, that those who gather from time to time to study such work gain that which cannot be bought with money and is without price. The development will and must come. Follow in the straight and narrow way and we will find the success in every manner.

Reading 254–90
Given on the Cayce Work

Then the purposes that there may be added moneys for the carrying on; let these not be first considerations but rather the help that may be given, the encouragement that may be given to those who have in one way or another contacted same. Let the spirit of the purposes and aims of the Association be manifested and expressed by those that would present same.

And if in the general order of conditions and circumstances the remunerations come that should be, then these may be used properly. For, as has ever been given, these will be supplied as fast as the individuals handling same *equip* themselves for their use!

Reading 1982–2
Adult Female

(Q) *How can I make a great success of life, become more spiritual and come in touch with those people and things and opportunities that will aid me in becoming a nobler and more successful woman, so I may be of more use in the world?*

(A) In all due consideration to the abilities of the body–mind, the body–consciousness of the entity, best that this be taken one at the time—and when the consciousness and the abilities of applying that cause, and that application brings more and more; for truly does the physical *or* spiritual *grow*; for, as has been given, grow in grace and in the knowledge of the truth, adding unto self those various forces of virtue, knowledge, temperance, long–suffering, patience, understanding, charity, love. All these, in their regular order. Be not unmindful that, as each is added in its own sphere and applied in self, that radiated will attract, and convince, and draw into the body that necessary to be accomplished by the body for a success. Do not look for success in dollars and cents and not in the spiritual life, for first *add* the spiritual life and *truly* all these things will be added unto you; for truly has it been said, seek the Lord while He may be found, adding unto self the various graces of the body–mind, the body–consciousness, and with these will come that success that is meted for the body. Be patient, and be long–suffering in the application—and often stand *still* and see the workings of the Lord! Do not *ever* attempt to *force* an issue! *Merit* that as would be attained by self, through meting that same element to each and every individual whom the entity may—or does—contact. Not a hard condition—not a hard element—and the body—*body*–mind—may say "these things have I always done but they do not bring me what I desire." Take, then, an inventory of self and see if *spiritually* these have been applied in the spiritual way and manner, and *not* applied spiritual laws expecting the physical results! First obtain the spiritual response and the physical is the natural consequence of same.

(Q) *Can I still make a success of my voice as to singing in public? How?*

(A) By applying. Any attainment may never be accomplished save by application. The body has the abilities, physically and mentally, yet builds such a wall within and about self—by fear—*fear*—that the application even of the talents within self are belittled by self, and others see the same result.

Reading 257–182
44-Year-Old Sales Manager

If each soul would understand what that means, he may pattern his life, his associations, his dealings with his fellow man, in such a way and manner as to make not only harmony and peace within his own home, his own mind, but all who contact the body-entity will know same for the beauty of his dealings with his fellow man in every way and manner.

Man should learn—[257] should learn—it is God that giveth the increase. Man as he labors, as has been given of old, is worthy of his hire. To take advantage, then, of an employee because of circumstance, because of surroundings—or for the employee to take advantage of the employer because of any condition that arises—must be met in the experience of them all.

For it is the law; and the law shall not pass away until it is fulfilled to every whit and every tittle in the experiences of each individual!

Hence the warnings given, that there be the building within self of that as would be not merely an axiom but as a living experience.

For the Lord thy God is a living God. Man's soul, man's activity, is a living experience. Begin to build constructively in the beginning, if you would have the success in all phases of the endeavor.

Reading 2506–1
54-Year-Old Female, Psychic

Ready for questions.

(Q) How can I be of greater service?

(A) As has been indicated; being true to self and to thy purposes, thy desires.

(Q) How can I benefit myself financially?

(A) Let this be rather as the outcome. For, know—the silver and the gold are the Lord's, and He withholdeth nothing that is good from those who serve Him. In service there is peace, and harmony.

Reading 585–12
47-Year-Old Female

(Q) *At [patient]'s death Miss [5223] has offered me a home with her. Shall I accept her offer? Is it indicated that she will ever marry?*

(A) This is attending to propose or to indicate ideas or minds in the future. This is not to be given. Use that in hand from day to day. Is the prayer for the bread of '46 or '47, or for today?

(Q) *Is there any way I can add to my income now?*

(A) It is sufficient unto the day. As there is the opportunity to use same, it will be given, and it will be prepared—a way for thee. There are ways, but let them present themselves as self makes self more gratified or contented where it is. Do not become too satisfied but make self content.

Reading 2497–3
22-Year-Old Female

(Q) *Will I be married within the next year?*

(A) If so desired.

(Q) *Do I know the person I am to marry? If not, when will I meet him?*

(A) That is of the entity's own making, and of the entity's own desire.

(Q) *Will I have financial and material comfort?*

(A) Would the entity have financial and material comfort, add that to self first that merits same, and through same may the entity be very sure—for, as has been given, "I will not forsake those who do my biddings," for those who serve God in the fullness of life have ever had, as *ever* will have, the gifts—the best gifts—in life.

Reading 1971–1
40-Year-Old Female, Widow

Hence the first injunction would be—Find within self what is thy desire and purpose. Not merely material—for the material things and material positions should be the outgrowth, the result; and not the whole purpose of an experience.

For they that love Him have the promise that they *shall* be clothed, they *shall* not want for food nor sustenance of the body.

Then, these supplied—as they may be in the experience—there should be a greater desire to so live that ye may constrain those whom ye meet day by day to glorify Him; not by precept alone, not by merely laudation, but by example; sowing those things in thy life that are as the fruits of the spirit—faith, hope, love, kindness, gentleness, patience, brotherly love. And if ye have these, ye are secure and safe in the promises of Him—who is the Prince of Peace—not of the world as the world knows the world, but He that *overcame* the world! And so may ye overcome the world—in His promises.

Reading 1947–1
31–Year–Old Female, Music Teacher

(Q) *Should I continue with my school or choir, or both?*

(A) Both.

(Q) *Should I write? If so, what?*

(A) By all means! those things pertaining to the bodily developments of individuals for special service and activities in the affairs of men!

(Q) *What should I do to draw an abundant or sufficient financial income to take care of my needs and opportunities for my children, and thus eliminate financial worries?*

(A) As ye apply thyself in the training of the children of others, as well as thine own, ye will find there will come the supply of the material things; for as ye give, ye receive.

Reading 4353–3
20–Year–Old Female, Actress

(Q) *If this body, [4353], fitted for the work she is now doing? If not, what work, to bring her material gain, would she be better suited for?*

(A) She, [4353], is especially fitted for the work she is developing toward, and the present is the means of development to make the success the body desires.

Do that.

(Q) *If fitted for her present work, how, or what, should she do to secure greater success, or a better part in her present production?*

(A) Give self wholly to the work in hand, keeping the mental and the physical fit for the spiritual development that may come through giving one's best to that in hand, for in the present we find the entity

developing toward the better parts that will come with the remunerative elements as developments progress.

(Q) *If not fitted for her present work, how may she secure success in the work she is
best suited for?*

(A) As given, labor in the direction as given.

(Q) *Give us advice, counsel, and information that will help encourage and be of
practical assistance to the body, [4353], in her daily work and development on this
earth's plane.*

(A) As given, the body needs keep the correct incentive in its work.
The body physically, mentally, spiritually, is peculiarly, particularly, sufficiently, evidently, fitted for the work as is before the body at present.

Then, enter in same with the whole heart, soul and body, knowing
that the laborer is worthy of his hire and that success will crown the
efforts when all is kept in the spirit of truth, and all must correlate one
with the other. Not in the effect of eye-service but as giving to those
that behold in the entity's labors that in the physical body exemplified
in a manner and way that brings the better thought to the public and to
the minds in spirit and in truth.

Follow in that way and we will come to the success that is desired in
the body, remembering what the price must be paid for a success and
the price is of self in mind, in spirit, in body.

Reading 5398-1
10-Week-Old Male

Does mankind consider he is indeed his brother's keeper? And this is
the manner in which man may answer the question. There will be no
want in bread for mankind when mankind eventually realizes he is
indeed his brother's keeper. For the earth is the Lord's and the fullness
thereof, and the bounty in one land is lent to man to give his brother.
Who is his brother? Our Father—then each of every land, of every color,
of every creed is brother of those who seek the Father, God. This instill
as ye interpret. Be faithful to the trust given thee.

Reading 815-3
32-Year-Old Male

(Q) *How can I shoulder responsibility with more grace and ease and poise, and assurance?*

(A) Of thine self, thou may do little. Take the *Lord* in partnership with thee! But be honest with *Him* and with thyself, as you would have *Him* to be honest and sincere with thee!

This does not bespeak that self becomes the "goody-goody," or as one afraid to do this or that! *All* force, all power that is manifested in the earth, *emanates* from a spiritual or God-force—as it manifests. *Man* in his madness, or in his selfishness, *turns* same into that which becomes either as miracles in the experiences of man or crimes that make for the crying out of the people who heed not.

Know that the Lord *is good!*

And to do good, to be kind, to be gentle, to smile even when in pain, to look up when others are even tramping upon thine feet and give praise to Him in the inner self, is that He seeks for. And He has promised glory and honor to those who do such.

The *mysteries* of His love, man makes same. For He is not afar off, but within thine own heart. For thine body is indeed the temple of the living God. Dost thou keep it, and the mind, in the condition in which ye may entertain Him there?

Then, *do* that.

For as ye do it unto the least or the greatest, ye do it unto Him. For he that would be the greater among men is the servant of all!

(Q) What is the focal-point, the integrating point, of my mental life, or entire life? Should I be married as part of the integration? I am divorced since 1932 but "fear" return, as I haven't "ironed out" my own responsibilities and emotional problems clearly in my mind, nor in my emotions.

(A) Why do you suppose, then, that what has just been presented thee has been given?

Let this be in thy mind and in thine *heart*, and in thine inner self:

As has been given of old, "There is ever, *today*, set before thee good and evil, life and death—*choose thou!*"

In other words, if ye would have peace, if ye would "iron out" kinks, if ye would know your relationships to others, set in thine inner self as to what is thine ideal. What is thy purpose in life? Is it to *get*, through the attitude of "Gimmee—Gimmee—Gimmee!" or is it to *give—give—give!* If it is the latter, then there should be the knowledge and security from within as given of old:

"Let others do as they may, but for me—I will *know* the living God," that has promised, does promise to—and does—meet oft within the conscience, in the mind, in the heart of each and every soul that has purposed in itself to be, to do, to give of self in a service to its fellow man.

Then, let His promise remain. For, as He has given of old; There has never been one that loves the Lord begging bread; nor one that lives the life of love failing to find harmony and peace in the inner man.

Then, do that thou *knowest* to do *today! Tomorrow* will be given thee the next step to take.

Be patient; be gentle; be kind. Show brotherly love. For what ye sow, ye reap. What thou art today is because of what thou hast done *about* that which thou didst know towards doing good.

For time and space are naught, but to man's self—to man's gratification—they become as the marks upon the soul of man, as to those periods when the heart, body, mind, is opened to service. Self-sacrifice. "I, the Lord, hath said, I no longer seek sacrifice of animals or of goats or of bullocks or of rams." Ye cannot buy thy way into the grace of thy Lord, nor into those purposes in thine inner self—for they cannot be satisfied by self-indulgence nor self-gratification.

In that as ye would purpose to do, *use* not others for stepping upon their hearts or minds—because others may have used thee. Bear ye up under same, knowing:

The Lord is the avenger of those that misuse His love in their relationship with their fellow man. And He, the Lord—the *life* that is *within* thee; that is thinking, moving; the *being* within self—*is* the avenger; *not* self:

Glory in the Lord!

Reading 1151–24
50–Year–Old Male, Labor–Management Mediator

(Q) Is it wise and imperative at this time for me to reduce substantially my general expenses in the light of present and future trends, or will my income be adequate to provide all of my and my family's requirements, and an overflow with which to bless the world?

(A) This might be answered in just that as we have indicated time and again. Remember—Whose *is* the silver and the gold? And so long as the efforts of the entity towards his fellow man, towards his country, towards his God, towards his own self and family, are in keeping with that which is the purpose of the entity, there will be abundance—and an overflow for the opportunities of aiding, helping here and there where the mind and heart indicates.

Keep that whole trust in Him; of course, not in any excess of extravagance in any phase or direction—but there will be sufficient for the needs of all.

Reading 1598–1
67–Year–Old Male, Missionary

(Q) How can I make the most of my remaining years in service to my fellow man?

(A) As has been indicated, help here and there to make the paths straight; to light the light to those who sit in darkness; to raise the hopes of those who have been discouraged, in that those who love Him—their seed shall not beg bread.

This may be done in writing, in speaking, in *doing!* For the experience, or this or that influence ye have seen or may see, is not the important thing—but what have ye done, and what are ye doing, and what *will* ye do *about same!*

For to say to him that is hungry, "The Lord be blessed—be thou filled," fills not that desire; it does not bring the consciousness.

But to aid the individuals to find themselves, aiding them to find that which will fill and make *their* life experience as *one* with Him—these be thy missions, these have been and are thy purposes.

Carry on! Be not weary in well–doing . . .

(Q) Should I borrow money freely to finance the Cooperative Farms in Mississippi, when there is danger of another depression or recession?

(A) How gave He concerning that which is good business in relationships to such? If it is for the purpose of bringing hope and faith and love into the lives and experiences of those who are to be aided, then *whose is* the money! For, "The silver and gold is mine, saith the Lord, and the cattle on a thousand hills."

Show *forth* thy love to thy fellow man, by putting his trust in God! There will *be* then no recession for such.

Reading 1720–1
25-Year-Old Male, Osteopath

Use conditions, use those of every experience as a stepping stone for success; but *do not* make the mistake to feel that to make a *financial* success is to succeed in the best or the whole matter. While position, power, wealth, is to be sought, to be sure—but let these conditions be rather that of the result from service given in little things, service rendered to the fellow man; for know that he that lendeth aid in *any* manner with the proper purposes in view—that is, to give self *in* such a service to the fellow man—lendeth to the Creative Energy, that is able to give that as exalteth, that as bringeth understanding, that as bringeth for the self that contentment that makes for the personality that leadeth, the *individuality* that commandeth; for remember, this may be termed as a *true* definition of the two: Personality leadeth. *Individuality* commandeth; not as men call command, "obey" and he obeyth, through fear—but commandeth and commendeth, being nearer of the same term.

Reading 1946–1
44-Year-Old Male, Unemployed

Hence in thy dealings with thy fellow men, bring hope—not for that so much of the material gain, for the earth is the Lord's and the fulness thereof.

Then, live holy and right in His ways and purposes—the *supply*, the abundance will be the result of thy fulfilling the law of supply in the experience of someone else!

For as ye do it unto the least of His children, ye do it unto thy Maker; and He will not leave thee comfortless—neither will He allow thy seed to beg bread—if ye have lived in the way in which the *glory* of His purpose is a part of thy life.

Reading 2136–1
25-Year-Old Male, Teacher

Taking, then, all those influences—as that to which the entity may build in the present:

Use that thou hast in hand today; for, as the opportunity, as the time comes for the giving out, be sure it is ever seasoned well with the words of truth that make for developments in the experiences of others towards constructive influences leading to God—for he that abides in Him shall want for nothing.

Reading 5666–1
42–Year–Old Female

(Q) *Any other suggestions for the welfare of self and children, to insure them a livelihood and a home?*

(A) *Best* be to insure them a life of worth–whileness, rather than livelihood—for that comes of itself when the life is expended in the direction to make same, not as only of pleasant—but of being worth while; keeping in *those* channels, and in the exercising of a service to whatever source and whatever channel through which one would develop self; not as all for self, but rather self for all, in a service—and in a manner in keeping with a continuity of purpose in the direction of building, or of making for that of a worth–whileness towards *constructive* influences, rather than of those as would make for personal aggrandizement of interests or selfish motives.

Reading 2744–2
25–Year–Old Female

(Q) *Is there anything I can do to bring about a more friendly relationship between my parents and myself and family?*

(A) This condition enters into many varying relationships. The causes which are to some unreasonable; to others of a very definite nature. That which is to the body, individual, an irritation, may be overcome. That as is held as animosity in the eyes of others must be overcome within themselves. *Satisfy* self that the proper attitude is being taken by self as regarding the relationships, considering that *others* have the right of *their* opinion as well as self, and an amiable condition may be arrived at, one more satisfactory than existent at present. *Yet*, as to what the actions of *others* are may not be governed by the individual, other than *self's* own action as respecting same.

(Q) *How can I help my husband with his present work? And should he remain* with this company? If so, what means can he use to increase production and shipments?

(A) That should be decided by the husband as to remaining with the present company, or present association. With the proper attitude OF individuals, this may be made remunerative—but simply remuneration is not satisfying to the inner self. There must be rather the attitude of a life *worthwhile* to those whom the body would serve, and of worthwhile service being rendered, rather than first and foremost of a remuneration as would bring this world's goods; for moth and rust doth corrupt, even as an evil conscience does beguile the best of intent. In service, as relating to assistance to the husband, be that of the helpmeet as promised at the time when the body became one in purpose and intent.

(Q) Is it advisable to keep our home or sell it?

(A) Depends upon what the decision of the body would be. The home is valuable, and will increase. As to whether the body would expend service in present surroundings, keep it. If the body would remove *from* present surroundings, might be the better to keep or might be better to sell. That should be the decision in the own mind. The property is valuable, and would be more so as time goes on.

(Q) Will my husband's plan of bringing his brother to ... and starting him in the furniture business prove successful?

(A) Too many conditions to be considered to say as to whether successful or not. First and foremost the body may only *influence* individual. As to their making a success, or the venture being successful, is up to the individual.

(Q) Would it be advisable for my husband to take out more life insurance or cancel some of his present policies?

(A) Again that which should be determined by the individual. As to advisability of cancellation or of increase, this should be rather in keeping with the *abilities* of the body to provide that which the body wishes to provide in such a direction.

Reading 270–18
43–Year–Old Male, Accountant

(Q) In the life reading [270-15] made on March 26 and the subsequent reading of June 27, 1928, this entity was given as one preferring Self, while he that, is to be a

Leader with Vision and Power must in self be a Servant. You will state if the creative forces of this body has succeeded in applying corrective measures, that will now permit it to seek that place on this plane where the ability, knowledge and vision of the Entity may be exercised to the fullest extent, or, if the corrective measures applied have not been manifested at least partial improvement you will then give further enlightenment with helpful suggestions for complete accomplishment. Advise body further as to his locating in the East—if this is coming about properly, and how body should act respecting same.

(A) The measures as have been taken by the body are having their effect upon the body in *many* ways and manners. As has been seen by the body (mental)—and as will be experienced, and as a natural result of an individual who attempts to, or who does change the attitude from an inward urge—there comes those experiences wherein, apparently, this has come to naught. Or, as may be better illustrated by that which came to the Master: When there was the determination to set self apart for the manifestation of the Spirit of the Father, through *that* physical Being known as the Master, immediately there came the tempter, and through other channels there were offered those opportunities to achieve in *earthly* measures those very positions that the *spiritual* measures were attaining; yet, as seen, as is *known* by the life as is experienced by those that would make their lives as One with Him, the approach, the application, the intent and purpose, the reasoning, the seed from which a result was to be obtained, came for an improper source. Now, in the application to *this* individual, [270], the *start* is well! In the application, and in the temptations as will be set before the mental being, the body–physical, keep self in that way and manner as to know that, he that would be a leader must *show* himself a leader; he that would be friendly must *show* himself friendly; he that has ability must *show* ability; he that would succeed must pay that price upon *which* a *firm foundation* of the proper seed, the proper intent, the proper purpose, is set. For one to gain his soul he must *lose* same in service. For one to attain that which is of the earthly conditions, one of an executive position, he must *lose* himself in that to which he would attain. Knowing, then, that this may be lost in the *wrong* direction as well as in the right, as has been shown the entity—not, then, as an eye single to the laudation of [270], but rather as an eye single for service *rendered* by [270] to accord the better service to those whom such positions, such conditions, *must* needs come. With that continuation, with that purpose set before self, there will come those changes in the material position, material sense, which will bring a satisfying, and a satisfaction of a life, a service, being spent in the proper way and manner; giving to the body that of earth's storehouse in position, power, finance, and the *ability* (if applied properly) to *use* same aright. Do that!

Reading 5502–4
47–Year–Old Female

(Q) What advice should [5502] have to strengthen her in the trust she already has manifested to be successful with the work?

(A) None other than that as has already been given, as keep that faith, that hope, in ministering to others as ye would be ministered to in their own position. For as we keep the faith with others as is committed to us, others will keep the faith with us. This the principle: Do unto others as ye would have others do unto thee. Let there be light, in the light brings the life (light) and understanding.

(Q) Should [257] attempt to develop his commercial enterprises for the benefit of this work with assistance and cooperation of [5502], or keep these entirely separate?

(A) That should be dependent upon the aims and purposes of each and should be decided within self as to that that is to be consecrated in that direction. For as has oft been given, he that will not use that already in hand would not use same were it a hundred-fold more. In the use of that in hand, in the direction as is purported, whether it be mental abilities, physical abilities, or the spiritual forces or the commercial side of experience, use that in hand and the increase comes with the use.

(Q) Is there any other advice for [257] to be used tomorrow in the things he is interested in that might help us get started quicker?

(A) Start with what you have; don't depend upon tomorrow or next day. Start with what you have; that gives the increase. Also it gave as of old: take the shoes even off thy feet; take the rod that is in thine hand; though be directed when thineself, thine mind, thine body is consecrated to an ideal, the purpose must be right.

Reading 3479–2
28-Year-Old Female

Be patient with self first, then with others. For in the use of thy abilities in the urges from Venus, as well as Saturn, ye may control those about thee or those whom ye would attract to thee as thy friends, as thy associates in thy activities.

In the urges, then: Find first what is thine own ideal—spiritually, mentally, materially. Let the ideals of the material life (of which ye become so conscious at times) be the outcome of the application of self and not as that to be attained whether or no.

Know in what and in Whom ye believe. Then thy abilities to control, thy abilities to attract, thy abilities to contribute to the mental, spiritual and material welfare of others, of thy associates, of thy companions, thy friends, thy community, will be in the purposes of thy ideal and not in the purposes of the self alone.

Keep true to self and ye will not be false to any.

Reading 4264–1
Adult Female

(Q) *How can this body reach the highest mental and spiritual development, Mr. Cayce?*

(A) By the study of self first and make a personal application to self, then you will understand others.

(Q) *How can this body increase her finances to a marked degree to help and give happiness to others, Mr. Cayce?*

(A) Just as we have given here. Whenever we give assistance to others others will give assistance to us, give and take. Money is not all to strive for in this world. Let this body keep this in mind as well. There are other things more value than money—if one gains the whole world and loses itself it has not gained much.

5

●

Overcoming Financial Challenges

Reading 263–4
23–Year–Old Female

(Q) *Please advise me as to how my husband and I may act so that we may make this experience one of unity and harmony?*

(A) This is an experience when each must know that it is the cooperative association in the activities as one to another, that there is the duty, there is the love, there is the necessary association on the part of each. Give and take. As ye would be done by, do ye so to the other; and this will make for an experience of harmony that will become as a light to many.

(Q) *What can I do to help the financial condition of my family?*

(A) Remove any thought or purpose or cause of anxiety for self from the others, and there will be made the harmonious experiences that will aid self and others in *making* for the necessary *material* activities in the experience.

Reading 333–3
50–Year–Old Male, Sales Engineer, Follow–Up Reading

In giving that which may be helpful and beneficial at this time, well that the attitudes, purposes, aims and desires of the bodies be considered as respecting their purposefulness in the experiences through which each in their own way are passing.

As indicated, if each soul will but put its reliance in the Giver of all good and perfect gifts, there comes the appreciation in the experience that every trial, every condition, is that each soul may know that the promises of Him who gave, "If ye will be my people I will be your God" and that the vicissitudes, the temptations, are but those things that—if used aright—will strengthen that relationship.

Then, in making the material application in the daily toils, in the daily activities and the associations with those through whom there may come the worldly things necessary for meeting the daily obligations that arise in the experience of every individual, know that man—in whatever position he may occupy—may be turned by the influence of the spirit of truth into a channel to bring blessings, experiences, conditions worth while in the lives of those whom the Lord doth succor, and *through* such channels meet those needs necessary.

For, His ways are not past finding out. And no man that labors in the Father's vineyard is other than in the manner as He gave, that as each labored so was the hire meted out to all in the same manner as was held in the inmost soul of the laborer in *His* vineyard.

Then, in making the connections, the associations, the activities that will meet these conditions in the experience, do so in the attitude, "I am thine, O Lord. Use me where, how, and in the manner as Thou seest I have need of, for a better presenting, a better representative and channel of blessings to others in Thy name."

Ready for questions.

(Q) Regarding financial affairs, is [333]'s new business connection of such character as to make it worth while?

(A) Each association and each character of association may be MADE worth while; in as much as there is put in in self, and in the attitude as given, it may be made worth while.

Reading 3976-16,
"World Affairs" Reading on the General Economic Conditions

For to have, to know and not do, not to make practical, not to make active, becomes (such information) as stumblingblocks.

What read ye, how interpret ye that which prompted this land in its separating itself or binding itself for a functioning in the affairs, the experiences of man? What prompted that? What prompted that binding of themselves in an activity?

These become the basic forces in the economic relations of a peoples of any nation.

There has arisen and there is arising in the affairs and the experiences of man everywhere the necessity of there being not so much the consideration of a land as of all lands as a unit. For *mankind* is his brother, and thou *art* thy brother's keeper.

Reading 4163–1
60–Year–Old Male, Civil Engineer

(Q) *Regarding material affairs: What is the nature of the business in which I am engaged?*

(A) The constructive forces as related to the material conditions that influence people's lives.

(Q) *What shall I do to meet present depressed conditions?*

(A) This might be answered in the manner as has been indicated, that in *most* directions where changes have been necessary to be met there have been or are being such associations made as to meet or to fill those necessary requirements for the meeting of the conditions. Where there has been the necessity for the relieving of associations, these are being brought about in such a manner that they will have as little influence upon the *whole*, as to the associations, as may be expected. These are *being* met in a manner that will bring the most satisfactory conditions and results; for, as has been given, there has already begun that general trend that will make for not only individuals so adjusting themselves by their concept of valuations in the material, the mental and the spiritual influences in their lives, as to better meet the conditions that are before them in the economic influences, as well as economic conditions being so altered as to cause material changes in the early portion of the Fall of the present year, with the general trend for a normalcy by the Spring of the coming year.

Reading 1362-1
48-Year-Old Male, Executive Assistant

In Mercury we find one making for the high mental abilities; one becoming very capable in whatever field of activity or endeavor in which the entity's mental and soul self finds material expression.

Then to succeed or to make for more than what is ordinarily termed material success becomes the dominating force.

If there is the application of self in the proper directions, and if the influence of Will—the ever changing factor—is applied in constructive forces ever, in the moral, in the mental, in the material associations, we will find those abilities, those qualities that have been experienced and as developed in Mercury and in Jupiter becoming the dominating force.

Thus may there be brought in the material experience of the entity in the present the harmonious associations, material gains, and a constructive experience for the benefits and service of the many...

As to the abilities of the entity in the present, then, and that to which it may attain, and how:

As has been given, so great are the possibilities, so great are the abilities of the entity to accomplish—not merely materially, not merely mentally, but in the practical application of the spirit of truth; and yet at times these seem so far afield to the entity.

For the entity has in the turmoils that have arisen lost sight of the proper evaluation of experiences, of the activities in its relationships to individuals, to groups, and to those to whom there is a duty not only in self but that they, too, with whom the entity is associated, may know the truth that will set them *free* from worry, tears, sorrow, sadness! Not by the mere material things of life but that which has made and does and will ever make for harmony in the experience.

Then, first study to show thyself approved unto God within. *Know* ye may know Him within thyself. All power, all love, all faith, all hope, all honor, all grace, all mercy, is within Him—and He hath promised to meet thee within thine own *self*. Then as ye study to show thyself approved unto the better within thyself, He will show thee the way...

Thy field of service to thy fellow men, as has been indicated, becomes in the fields of communication; that deal with the radio and every form of communication; and a closer association with the national and international fields of operative forces will bring thee greater happiness in *lending* of thyself, for it becomes a portion of thyself—and will make for an outlet where the material gains may come.

But first *know* ye the Lord, for the cattle and the gold and the silver are His, and all ye have is lent ye of the Lord! Only that ye give away, of self, of money, of time, of patience, of love, do ye possess!

For if ye would have life, give life! If ye would have friends, *be* friendly! If ye would have loved ones, love others, do good to them though they may despitefully use you; for they did that unto thy Lord and Master.

In the application of self in the fields of activity, draw nigh unto that which is good and it will draw nigh unto thee.

Ready for questions.

(Q) Please advise me as to the present stability of my position with the ... Electric Co. Is there an opportunity to realize a satisfactory future there, or should I make a change?

(A) As we find, as has been indicated, this has been and may be used as a stepping–stone to greater opportunities, greater possibilities for the associations with communication fields rather than those of *commercial* lines in the electrical forces—that offer the greater opportunities. And ways and means are being opened that as we find will bring about an association of that nature.

For soon, as has been so oft given from here, there must be a closer association with the telegraph, the radio and the telephone communications.

Hence as all of these have been through the many ages, through the many experiences of this entity, this soul, thy study, thy desire, thy wishes, thy activity—to give expression in same in the present offers the greater opportunities for advancement materially. But in thine advancement let this warning be:

Think not only of material gains, but of how great a service ye may be to thy fellow man! For if ye serve the masses, the individuals, without thought of self save as for service, ye serve thy Maker.

(Q) Having desired to be re-associated with [...] with whom I was previously connected, when and how should I best continue my negotiations and contacts with [...]?

(A) As has been indicated, there are—as we find—those conditions being brought about in which there may be closer and better associations; and in the application of self greater opportunities. As to how soon, keep those negotiations open—and prepare self, in thought, in body, in mind, for ready, active service in same.

(Q) How can I best adjust my upset financial affairs due to the depression?

(A) Just as has been indicated again, go to those whom thou owest obligations—and those things that materially demand consideration. Give the explanation, give the thought to same. *Ask* and ye will receive the opportunities for being able to meet them in thy service for others.

Not speculating, not calling on advantageous positions that ye would clear self; but know, only they that are able to suffer are able to know glory, to know peace, to know harmony. These may sound at first only as idealistic sayings, but if ye turn within and ask of thy better self ye will find the answer there.

(Q) Would it be possible to negotiate some loan whereby these obligations can be pooled, rather than all mixed up?

(A) As we find, as soon as there is definite (and permanent) connection made with communications, this very condition *can* be consummated and give self the opportunity to meet same in a way and manner that would be satisfactory to all.

Reading 3577-1
56-Year-Old Female

Then, spiritualize and visualize purposes, in the manner in which the entity desires things to be done, and you'll have them done!

The entity need never worry about material things. It may worry about them for others, but why worry—when you can pray and have it! but you'll have to live like you pray! In thy spirituality don't begin to become one who would ruin [run?] to attain and then not use to the glory of that through which it may be presented.

Reading 3538-1
46-Year-Old Female, Music Teacher

In analyzing the physical and mental attitudes of the body here, [3538], we find that anxieties as to material things and conditions have had too great a stress put upon them by this body...

These should be thy first approach. For, as He has given, be not anxious wherewithal ye shall be clothed nor wherewithal ye shall be fed.

For, the Father knoweth that ye have need of these things. When ye apply the spiritual life in thy relationships to others, there will be the supply. For, does He not clothe all nature? Are not the silver and gold His? Then act in that manner!

Begin by reading Exodus 19:5, and know that it is meant for thee. Then read the whole of Deuteronomy 30, and know that the counsel is being given to thee, and that ye have to choose each day, now, and every other day. Don't say within self that these are of no avail to thee, but use them.

For again and again He says, "Try me—see if I will not pour out to thee a blessing."

Do that. Then as ye study, know that ye are not only read but apply John 14, 15, 16, 17. These are not merely words, they are living truths. He came that ye might have life and have it more abundantly. He withholds no good thing from thee, if ye will only choose it, live it. Live it in thy speech to others.

Though the heavens fall, though the earth be broken up, His promises will remain—and He will not fail thee, if ye fail Him not.

Reading 2897–4
35-Year-Old Male, Musical Conductor

(Q) *Why is Edgar Cayce surrounded by such wrong vibrations and entities in this great work?*

(A) For there has been the continued battle with those forces as Michael fought *with* over the body of Moses. He that leads, or *would* direct, is continually beset by the forces that *would* undermine. He that endureth to the end shall wear the Crown. He that aideth in upbuilding shall be entitled to that that he *builds* in his experience. He that faltereth, or would hinder, shall be received in the manner as he hinders.

(Q) *Why don't the Forces prevent continual financial annoyance to him?*

(A) That there has been set a monetary *standard* by many as to that which is of worth or is success, indicates the vibrations as well as the purpose of such. Not by might nor by power, but by 'My Word.' Not that man lives by bread alone, but by *every word* that is a promise to that man by or from the Creative Forces, or God. That that a man worships, *that* that man becomes.

(Q) What are the revelations as to why he is in difficulty?

(A) No difficulty exists in the man's soul. There exists difficulty in the minds of individuals who, with monetary *measures*, see all forces hindered as to their concept of success.

(Q) Since Virginia Beach was given as the proper place for the foundation of this work in the material world, why has not success come?

(A) He that looketh upon the monetary conditions as success looketh in vain! It *has* succeeded beyond measure in the spiritual forces, *is* succeeding in monetary or the pecuniary manner.

Reading 802–2
39-Year-Old Male, Manager, Engraving Company

In giving the mental and spiritual understanding or interpretations, that which is prompting in its activities in the earth, in the relationships to its own self, we find:

If it seeks for the soul development, then turn within. For, what may be given as truths, as axioms, as those influences that may make for the awareness of the divine, these become as sounding brass if there is not the desire, the impelling influence, the activity from within, to make manifest love—that makes for that which will exalt in the earth, in the relationships with the fellow man, that which is the ideal, the hope, the understanding of the entity.

When the ideal is founded in materiality, it is too oft found—when man has paid the price for fame, for fortune, for position, for power—that it is as naught; something lacking yet. Too oft is this found; unless that which is prompting the desire, the hopes, is founded in the spiritual life, in the inner self, as to the glory of that which gives life itself. With this as the prompting, though, one may find peace and harmony, and that which passeth understanding in *whatever* realm is necessary, for the advancement, for the making aware of that in the experience—of that abiding grace—that comes from living that even as He gave, "As ye would that men should do to you, do ye even so to them." For this is the law from the beginning. As ye manifest, not to an unseen God, not simply to that necessary for the laying aside of those things that make for satisfactions in the material life, but glorifying them. For the purposes are the glorifying of Him. For he that seeketh the Lord and findeth

Him shall have "all these things added" as it becometh necessary.

Be patient; be kind; show brotherly love. Making for those things that are of the spirit becometh, then, the basis for the activities in the earth, and His promises are faithful that, "Ye abiding in me, I in the Father, ye shall ask in my name and it will be done unto thee." Even the desire of thy heart concerning thy spiritual life.

Ready for questions.

(Q) *I have been working literally day and night to build an organization of capable, decent people. Each time I bend over backward to help someone in distress and manufacture a good job for them I am condemned by others. And, generally, I find I am later condemned by the person helped. Is it worthwhile to continue or should I judge entirely by sad past experience?*

(A) What matter though the man lose the world if he gains his own soul? Patience maketh one aware of his soul. As ye deal to others, so will it be dealt to thee. This is the unfailing, the unfaltering principle, the law—*love*. As ye seek, as ye do, though the whole *world* condemn thee, though the others forsake thee, forsake *not* those principles that make for the satisfying of that thou hast set, thou dost set as an ideal! Be *patient* and ye shall see the glory of the Father manifested in the lives, not only of those that have condemned or do condemn thee for thy singleness of purpose but in doing that which maketh for oneness in thy relationships to thy fellow man ye shall *see* that they—thy efforts—shall not, will not, go unrewarded in *any* direction. Be patient.

First learn to be patient with self, then ye will know patience with thy fellow man. *Give* thy work—thy relations with thy fellow man, *in* thy work—a *soul*, as it were, or the awareness that honesty, truth, justice, mercy are those things that *will* and *do* build in every field of activity.

(Q) *The firm I am working for put me off from time to time on my requests for a reasonable return for time and effort expended in their behalf. Have I made a mistake in not looking elsewhere for another position, or should I continue my efforts for recognition here, and how should I go about it?*

(A) Continue the efforts for recognition here. Let the activities be towards a service to thy fellow man in the field of thy choice, whether with those in authority or those that would aid in thine efforts; and ye shall find that as there is the word of self—not by mere rote but by thy activity, by thy own association; not only with those in authority but those that ye serve—it will make for those returns not only as commensurate with the efforts that ye have and do put forth, but shall bring forth forty, yea sixty and a hundred fold for thy labor—*if* it is given in love!

(Q) *I have had the blues many times and have been wondering if it might be a natural circumstance due to general conditions or if it could partially be caused by a physical condition. Please explain.*

(A) As one allows self to be overcome by those things that oppress or depress, as one gets more and more of the *feelings* of unappreciation on the part of others, these are as the crushing of one's own egotism in the *mental* phase or portion of the experience of an entity. As one finds such expressions become more and more a portion of the material or physical self, there is produced then a physical reaction. Not as other than a mental aptitude as respecting same; but when these conditions approach thee (for all are as upon the wheel of life), look rather within than without. And in thy activity give praise to someone, even though it be a feeble effort on the part of such an one. Find those that are also as thyself bemuddled by the cares of the world, the deceitfulness of man's voice, the inexpressionness of man's association and activity. Give not away to the satisfying of thine own indulgences and say, "What's the use; no one cares!" If thou dost not care for thyself, who may care for thee?

Then, let such experiences be rather those periods when ye would in some other's life, not thine own, make it a period of joy. And ye will find that such will pass away, even as the morning dew when the light of truth and justice and mercy shines out upon those things; for they shall become as high points of thine own experience and not that of despondency, despair or the blues. Do not mistake the blues for a grouch, and a grouch for the blues. But let thy yeas be yea and thy nays be nay with thy *real* inner self. And look to that from within. For He, thy God, thy better self, thy inner man, thy Christ Consciousness, thine own soul, hath promised to meet thee there—and to guide thee in all things that will make for making thine experience in the earth not only a joyous one but more and more worthwhile for those that thou dost contact day by day. And thy light, thy word, shall *shine*—if ye will but enter in!

(Q) *Have I the proper mental and physical qualifications to succeed as an executive?*

(A) You have the mental and physical qualifications to succeed, if ye will but look within. Who is the greater executive than thy God? Who may guide thee aright greater than He? What thou lackest He may add to thee, if ye seek in that manner. For His promise has been, "If ye will be my children, I will be thy God, and I will raise thee up that none shall say aught against thee, and those that would hurt or make thee afraid shall become as naught." *Stand* with thy loins girded about with the *truth*, putting on the armor of God; and thou shalt be strong in thy might!

Reading 700–1
45-Year-Old Female

(Q) *How can I save my home and overcome the unhappy condition that has almost wrecked me?*

(A) This, to be sure, can only be accomplished first in the controlling of self and of self's emotions, that have been magnified by the associations and the activities in the experience of the body. For, through those regular channels that are set for the financial activities or associations in the body may this portion be attained.

But in the mental attitudes, the mental associations, know first (and repeat this in self until there is the conviction and the knowledge within self that it is a portion of thine *own* experience): *nothing*, physically, mentally or spiritually, may be taken *from* thee that is truly thine, that thou hast gained through thine own mental and spiritual activity—lest thou *alone* cast it aside!

(Q) *How can I regain my voice as a singer?*

(A) Those conditions in the physical that have prevented, do prevent the full activity of the attributes of the body, *will* be restored in the *correcting* of the physical disturbances of the body. Then by singing or pouring out the soul; not to be seen of others, not to satisfy alone self's own laudation or even audition, but as to make—*through* the application of self—that channel which will bring to others something that is helpful and hopeful in their *own* experience. And this will bring to self, to others, *contentment* and peace and harmony, as little else can. Not for self; for others!

(Q) *Shall I go to Francis and live with him?*

(A) Weigh these conditions well in thine own experience. As we see in the present, it would be well.

Keep that faith, that simplicity of trust that thou once had in those influences within self that prompted thee in thine activities; and ye shall find—will find—that His strength, that comes to those who put their trust in Him, may be truly within. Get self and self's own material desires rather in that position of being used as helpfulness, hopefulness to others, and thou wilt find rest from the strifes, the turmoils that have disturbed the mental body. For the abilities are within thee, the opportunities are before thee; turn them not aside. Give the body and all its attributes a more perfect channel of beauty of expression in all thine associations with others, and ye will find ye have made a choice that will bring happiness in thine experience.

Reading 585–4
40-Year-Old Female

(Q) *Must I experience the loss of my home? If not, how can I save it? How can I meet the payments before they foreclose?*

(A) As we find, in making for those associations and connections and making some concessions in self and in self's relationships, these may be divided in ways and means and manners that will not necessarily call for the losing of the home.

But know that those things that are lost were never thine; only that thou hast given away is thine!

(Q) *Why is it that money slips away from me so easily and I can't meet my obligations?*

(A) This may be found if there is the study of those experiences of self in those associations where so easily were the material things a part of that activity wherein the spending of same brought so much disturbances to others. And this then is being met in that so easily do those little confusions come that call for the use of the material things, for the gratifying of those conditions and experiences for the moment.

Learn ye the lesson, and be patient!

Reading 303-13
49-Year-Old Female, Bookkeeper

(Q) Please give me any other advice I may need at present.

(A) Do not allow disturbing conditions to so *fret* the body–physical as to undermine or to sap the vitality. *Know*, as has oft been given, in thine own *strength alone* little may be accomplished, but in the strength of the power and the might of thine Savior, in and through His promises, *much* may be done. Not to sit still but as He hath given, ye see about thee in thy daily associations, in thy home, in thy friendships, in thy relations, the harvest already white and there needs be rather those that would work in His vineyard. And His promises are as they have ever been, sure—that the just, neither the children of the just, shall beg bread; neither shall want or need come nigh unto those that seek to be a channel of manifestations of His love among His people.

Reading 254-11
Given on the Cayce Work

(Q) In consideration of the fact that Edgar Cayce is devoting his entire time to the work, give the reason for his not being able to obtain sufficient financial support for him and his family's material sustenance, and how may he, Edgar Cayce, correct this condition?

(A) Live closer to Him, who giveth all good and perfect gifts, and ask and ye shall receive; knock and it shall be opened unto you. Give and it shall be returned fourfold. Give, give, give, if you would receive. There has never been the lack of necessities, neither will there be, so long as adhering to the Lord's way is kept first and foremost.

Reading 254-43
Given on the Cayce Work

(Q) How shall the Board raise the necessary funds to supply money to pay salaries and the immediate overhead of the Association?

(A) Dig in! and *begin*. With the beginning, as has ever been—and will be—will be that sufficient for the care or needs. For "The silver and the gold is mine," saith the Lord, and "I will recompense him who would serve in that that would make thine brother nearer to that understanding of the relationship of man to man and man to the Maker."

Reading 254–64
Given on the Cayce Work

In this respect, then, we find there is constantly occurring shortages. Hence, there must be that there is a fault in some direction.

Then, analyze same in accordance with the manners that have been given that this should be presented; and there will be, there should be, those sufficient returns, then, for the carrying on of every phase of the endeavor in the present.

The first consideration, then, is:

Is the good being accomplished? Yes.

Is there sufficient remuneration from that being accomplished? No.

Then, wherein does the fault lie? There is too much period when good might be obtained, that there are vacant periods. Then, not *sufficient* numbers that may be served are being served! Wherein does such a fault lie?

In that there has not been the efficient organization that has been indicated, that there might be every period possible filled.

Then, wherein does the fault lie in this direction?

In that those who have been aided have not been sufficiently urged toward their endeavors in interesting others to gain for themselves that which might be accomplished in their experience; for, as given, the development primarily for individuals through associations with the work, or *this* work, should be *self*-development, or the development toward the *ideal* set by the Association that *fosters* the work!

Then, there needs be that there be better cooperation in individual activity, in the group activity, and that the stress be for a sufficient number to continually seek through this channel for that which may be gained in their individual experience, for the carrying on of the work.

When this has been accomplished, it will be seen that there is sufficient for all.

That there have arisen conditions in the *immediate*, now, that are out of the ordinary should be sufficient evidence that the faith, the confidence, the experience in those that are *immediately* affected is either faltering or that sin, of some character or nature, is at the base of the conditions.

Be not impatient. Remember that these are the crucial tests of a

people called for, and to, a service that may aid in keeping such a balance as to preserve for the coming ages that hope in Him, that may be
sustained by the faith in those that suffer in body—and who are in the
present *denying* the desires, the needs, and are even being scoffed at for
their belief in those things that are as old men's fables, as children's
fairy tales, as unbalanced individuals wander in their meditations; yet
the answer is in the results, for "By their fruits ye shall know them." And,
the fruits *first* must be the *mental* and *spiritual* attitudes created in the
hearts and minds of those that seek through these channels; and, though
there be tarryings in the present in the physical and material things,
these *must* be the eventualities—and will begin now.

Reading 254-79
Given on the Cayce Work

How much suffering there is! And how happy those should be that
have been called to a purposefulness in relieving suffering physically,
and most of all in bringing and in giving hope to those who find life's
pathway in the material world beset with shadows and doubts and
false hopes.

Give ye thanks for *thy* own calling; for whom He has loved He has
predestined—and ye are in thine own light when ye allow the foibles of
material things to hinder in thy application of that *thou knowest* to do.

Report of Reading 254-79

Gladys Davis note: We interpreted this [volunteered reading 254-79]
to be a message of encouragement to the staff, especially to Edgar Cayce
and Gertrude Cayce who were concerned over finances and inability to
keep up monthly payments on their home. Interestingly enough, when
Baldwin Brothers had the property re-surveyed with the idea of refi-
nancing it, discovery was made that the house was built half on the lot
next door, not even owned by the loan company. This worked out beau-
tifully for the Cayce family, because it took the loan company almost a
year to get everything straightened out [to quietly buy the lot on which
the other half of the house rested, etc.] and during the interim no payments needed to be made.

Reading 254–85
Given on the Cayce Work

(Q) *Is it not a proper purpose of the Foundation to bring to Mr. Cayce sufficient and abundant material substance to free him from the necessity of the routine of two readings a day under which he has hitherto been forced to function in order to merely provide his living?*

(A) Well from that angle. Rather learn ye that in making such provisions in the material and the mental, and in making for those things, not merely two but many such approaches may be made. *Remember*, my children, it is the *fear* of the material conditions that wrecks the material body. It is the *fear* of this or that, that prevents a channel from making for the greater supply.

(Q) *Should not the resources of all the earth be at his command from now on so that the Father's Kingdom on earth may speedily arrive?*

(A) These arise, my children, in the hearts and minds of those that are aided. It is rather in thine hands that ye make those that have received and do receive of the crumbs, of the glory, of the bounty, become aware of *their* position in same.

(Q) *Will it be in accord with the Father's Will from now on for Mr. Cayce to use his powers to draw to the Foundation adequate financial substance for the support of his and the Association's spiritual activities?*

(A) Things that are of the spirit must arise from the spiritual promptings; things that are material arise from the material promptings. What seek ye? Remember, my children, those examples shown thee. What spoke the Lord? Know ye not that where thy burdens have been as those of the finger, they shall become as thick as the thigh? Know ye not that those that seek material things must in all things pay the price of same?

(Q) *To this end will it be well for Mr. Cayce to assist in the development and manipulation of natural resources or of business through the cooperation of business associates who could be called together for his purpose?*

(A) Seek ye these as through the purposes of each, and when same are called for such purpose. For there is a way that seemeth right unto a man but the end thereof is death.

In seeking, then, know that what is the Lord's is to be used in that direction. *Whose* is the storehouse, the Lord's or man's? Who doth His biddings? The Lord man's biddings or the man the Lord's biddings?

Keep thou, then, that way open for those warnings that ye may search and find in the experiences of those that would make of themselves as glorious in the sight of men, that they would glorify the Lord the more. Use rather, my children, that thou hast in hand. For what said He? *"Surely the ground upon which thou standest is holy."* For he that hath dedicated his life, his service, his ability, is called of the Lord. What hast thou in thy hand? Cast it from thee that thy hand, thy mind, thy soul, may be awakened to Him who maketh for the increase in the experience of every soul! Man may sow, man may water, man may nurture; yet only God may give the increase. Whosoever doeth that which may make for a questioning in his purposes before man, or before God, is judged of same. Let thy light shine where ye are! Be ye not impatient. For the Lord is not mocked; and whatsoever man soweth, that must he reap. For it is line upon line, precept upon precept, here a little, there a little—and in His own time.

Reading 254–95
Given on the Cayce Work

Keep the ways thou hast set before thee. Know in what manner ye have attained. Know that though there are turmoils, know that though there are discouragements, the earth is the Lord's, the silver and the gold, the cattle on the hills. They are thine, then; use them in thy daily living in such a manner that they bring not to thee but to others that love you would have the Father show thee. For that ye give, that alone ye have. That ye lose ye never had. That ye spend or abuse, ye do so only to thine own consternation.

Reading 294–41
48–Year–Old Male

As is necessary for the entity, there will be supplied, through self and through these forces as pertain to association with same in the forces of Edgar Cayce, as manifested in the material world, will be given that necessary, then, for that correct manner to supply that necessary for the building of the work in the financial manner, through the various changes as will be seen that come from time to time, see? There will be many various things, see, that will be presented, and in various manners will they come, see, for as has been given, "Ask and ye shall receive. Knock and it shall be opened to you," see? and as the conditions arise, keeping then, both, in that way and manner that is holy and acceptable unto Him, the Giver of all good and perfect gifts. The supply will come from that storehouse that is of His building, for none will suffer in the following of that way that leads to life eternal. For the physical must be supplied with those necessary elements of life and sustenance to be able to comprehend, to gain, the full and unexplorable conditions of the spiritual force manifest in the material world.

Be thou faithful, then, guided, guarded, directed, by Him.

Reading 657–3
Adult, Male, Osteopath and MD

(Q) What can I do personally to help improve my financial condition?

(A) That these conditions have in the past offered, and do in the present offer great obstacles from the human or the material standpoint is obvious. But he that considereth the body and the attributes of same first, chooseth unwisely. That these must be met for the peace of the mind is a portion of that which must be met in that holy of holies, and *there*—and there alone should the entity, the body, the mind, find the answer. There is in the very make–up of the body–mind the speculative instinct, or fact. Facts in the material must be met by material situations. Facts in the mental must be met by the mental and the reason. And those that seek for spiritual life in material things are following after folly. But those that seek in the spiritual the mental *and* the material expressions of self and associations, are wise! Hence, then, use that thou hast in hand. Be guided to put the proper evaluations, the proper stress where it—the stress—is due; and ye will find that thou wilt be guided in doing those things that are for the best. There are to come, and are eminent in the experience of the entity in speculative channels, those periods when those that seek such shall be the material gainers; and these are in those specific fields of activities in the utilities of this and of other great nations. And by the indulgence in same there may come those material gains. But they that live by such shall die by such. For they that live by the sword must abide by the sword's decision. They that live by the spirit shall be alive indeed! And yet these are a portion of the entity's experience. How, first, will ye use that which has and that may come from the use of the material gains? How hast thou used them in the past? Art thou worthy in thine own meeting with thy Lord in His holy place to claim that thou may be entrusted with ten talents when thou hast used two badly? Hast thou the claim that thou may be given fifty talents when ten have been mislaid?

When ye have found grace and favor in Him that is the Father of mercy and peace and harmony and understanding, *then* these will be given thee in these fields. Calumet, to be sure, is ripe for many decisive changes that may come both ways, but as to how—Let the Lord thy God tell thee; not of silver, not of gold, but the God that stands with thee as thou standest for thy brother in the day of need, and when and as thou showest mercy so will it be shown thee!

(Q) *Do you find that it would be advisable for me to share professional offices with another doctor?*

(A) Provided these are, of course, in such accord that their purposes, their aims, their desires, their policies—yea, even in more material their tactics—are compatible.

(Q) *Whom would you advise?*

(A) Any of those associations where these are to be had. For, as is the experience of the entity from all of its approaches to the true spiritual natures of things, as ye seek, as ye send out in and through thine inner self those needs, *who*—who is the provider? Though man in his strength and in his wisdom may work, labor, toil, who giveth increase? Who pointeth the way? Who bringeth it to pass in thine experience? Art thou, wilt thou keep in that way? Then these may be brought about—the correct ones, the correct understandings.

(Q) *Would you advise that I seek to make such a change, and when?*

(A) By the first of the year.

(Q) *Should I change my professional location of offices?*

(A) Of course, these may be answered in the same way and manner—as one seeks truly within the self. This is only bantering questions, when we consider what has just been given thee as the basis of truth wherein a life, an experience, a soul, an entity, may find the answer to any question that may arise within its own experience. How, ye may ask, is the step by step in which I may find such an answer? First, in thine meditation ask the material mind, is it yes or no—and thou wilt receive the answer; as a vision, as a word. Then take it to thine inner self and let the answer be given thee then from within. And thou wilt *know*, and thou wilt it be made aware within every fibre of thine body. For, as ye well know, my son, in thine inner self, each atom of thy body *must* coordinate, *cooperate*, one with another, that ye in thine physical begin may have health, or even balance that thy mind, thy entity—yea, thy soul-body—may have the better channel in which to serve. For indeed thine body is the temple of the living God. If thou hast desecrated it, or dost discrete it, what is the answer?

Reading 2533-7
38-Year-Old Male, Insurance Agent

(Q) *Outline and explain a method or technique of effective prayer as to apply the laws of increase and to overcome the laws of gravity by these entities.*

(A) As ye are in and under, and apply laws, ye become the law. As He applied the law—that is, as Jesus, the man, that is in relationship to thyself—as He applied the law He made Himself equal with the law, by becoming the law. No doubt, no fear, no animosity, no self—but selfless in God's purpose. This overcomes the law as related to all phases of materiality, including gravity, including supply, including *all* phases of the experience in the earth.

(Q) *Explain repentance and remission of sins as they apply to us.*

(A) Repentance means being sorry, as He, as He wept with the young man who turned away when he was told, "Sell all thou hast and give to the poor, and follow me." He was sorry for the young man. Why? As He gave, "Thou art not far from the kingdom of God." In other words, "Thou art not far from being wholly the law," but the fear of lack, the fear of the lack of the medium of exchange—or of wealth—hindered.

As in thine own experience—in these two—the desire to know His biddings, realizing there is a purpose that is a union of strength in each, is as that same question asked by that man. The sorrow was not of the man but of Jesus, who became the Christ.

Repentance, then, is "Not my will but Thine, O Lord, be done in me, through me, day by day."

Then, let the prayer of each be—three times each day—agree upon a time—not merely say it, but feel it, be it:

"Lord! Thy will be done in me, today. Lord, Thy will be done in me, today."

Then, as ye go about thy daily tasks, in associations with others, let thy words, thy acts, thy thoughts, be ever, *"Lord, Thy will be done in me, today."*

This does not mean that there is to be long-facedness, but *joy*—even as in Him when He wept with those that wept and rejoiced with those that did rejoice; even supplying the wine, even of greater flavor and potency than the bridegroom was able to supply.

He was *all* things to all men. Ye, under His direction, by that constant prayer, may be—daily—all things to all men. Thus will each soul be *glad*, be *joyous*, in thy coming, and sorrow at thy going.

Reading 996–10
Given on Financing the Cayce Work

(Q) Should we stay for further development here, or should we return to Virginia Beach and take up the work where we left off?

(A) The work is not left off! This is improperly worded—for work only progresses, and—as has been given—first to individuals, then to groups, to classes, to masses, to nations, to peoples. Just as is seen that the work has progressed since the use of same applied to assisting those that would gain a better understanding or conception of the purpose of life, and the applying of the purpose in the lives of individuals—whether for mental, moral, spiritual, or financial gains. In the present, then, we find work incomplete. This should first be set aright, and then in the next five to six—not later than eight days—return; and let each as has contacted and associated self in mind, heart, body, or money, so apply those conditions as have contacted their lives to bring to themselves and to others the reward of the contact of association in the broader, greater, better sense, of having seen the manifestations of the Universal law as applies in human lives.

(Q) How may we help to set this right?

(A) By giving just that information that, as it were, each may be pricked in their own hearts, as to apply the purpose of life in their individual lives and association with men. Return then in eight days, see?

(Q) *What should we do regarding our financial condition at this time, taking into consideration our obligations and expenses?*

(A) The laborer is ever *worthy* of the hire. The conditions as relating to finances take care of themselves, when individuals apply themselves in the way and manner as is in keeping. Fear not! for consider the lilies of the valley, or the grass that is abloom to-day and to-morrow cast in the oven—for "The silver and gold is mine," sayeth the Lord, and he that would harken and do according to the ways as is set shall never athirst nor want for bread.

Reading 262–77
Study Group Reading, Lesson on "Destiny"

Then, today, will ye not rededicate thyself, thy body, thy soul, to the service of thy God? And He that came has promised, "When ye ask in my name, *that* will be given thee in the earth." Then, do not become impatient that ye are counted in this day as a servant, as an humble worker, as one that is troubled as to food, shelter, or those things that would make thy temporal surroundings the better. For ye grow weary in waiting, but the Lord will not tarry; eternity is *long*, and in that ye may spend it in those things that are joy and peace and harmony, make thy self sure in Him. How? "As ye do it unto these, my brethren, ye do it unto me." Just being kind! Thy destiny is in *Him*. Are ye taking Him with thee in love into thy associations with thy fellow man, or art thou seeking thy *own* glorification, exaltation, or thine own fame, or that ye may even be well-spoken of? When ye do, ye shut Him away.

Enter thou into thy chamber not made with hands, but eternal; for there He has promised to meet thee. There alone may ye meet Him and be guided to those things that will make this life, now, happiness, joy and understanding.

As ye have received, love ye one another even as He has loved you, who gave up heaven and all its power, all its glory, that thine mind can conceive, and came into the earth in flesh that ye through Him might have the access to the Father, God. In Him there is no variableness or shadow made by turning. Then, neither must thy thoughts or thy acts cause a frown or a shadow upon thy brother—even as He. For He gave, "Be ye perfect, even as thy heavenly Father is perfect." Ye say, "This cannot be done in this house of clay!" Did He? Ye say, "This is too hard for me!" Did he grumble, did He falter? To be sure, He cried, "Father, if it be possible, let this cup pass." Yea, oft will ye cry aloud, even as He. Ye cannot bear the burden alone, but He has promised and He is faithful, "If ye put thy yoke upon me, I will guide you."

Then, when we come in our sorrows alone and there comes the peace, the quiet, and then those periods of joy and gladness when we forget— we carry the thought of others, of those that would make merry, and wonder why the joy has passed. It is because we have left Him outside.

Take Him, then, in thy joys, in thy sorrows, in *all* of thyself; for He alone hath the words of life.

6

●

Miscellaneous Advice from the Edgar Cayce Readings

Reading 1587–1
43-Year-Old Male

For peace, harmony, things that are known as material gains must be the result of honest effort, honest desire in the direction of being creative in relationships to others; rather than the result of getting while there is the ability for it to be obtained without thought of the source—for this can only bring canker and rust and those things that create fear in the minds and experiences of others.

Reading 1435–1
43-Year-Old Female

(Q) *Are there any savings accounts or deposit boxes left by my late husband, [...] in Canada, that I may be advised of at this time through this channel?*

(A) In the Trust Company in Montreal. Seek there through the same channels that may be set in motion, and you will find some that are worth while and of interest.

(Q) *Is there anything that I can do regarding the Insurance Trust left by my former husband, [...], and handled by the First Central Trust Co., in ..., Ohio?*

(A) Only through those same channels in which there will be set in motion, and are being set in motion, the activities of unraveling all of the concerns of the late [...].

(Q) Any suggestions or advice regarding handling the affairs of my late husband's estate and securing that which is rightfully mine, especially regarding property owned?

(A) These as we find must be accounted for to those in authority, as has been set in motion, and as has been given—the lending of self to those in giving all the information and keeping those things alive will offer the channels through which there may be obtained that *justly* thine.

The whole purpose, then, is:

What *will* be done by self with that so obtained? Use not as in self-aggrandizement, self-indulgence, nor in such measures that it is not appreciated by those channels in which it may be handled.

But be thou close to Him; for the silver and the gold is the Lord's, and that which will come into thine experience is *lent* thee. Ye would not rob the Lord!

(Q) Please explain what is meant by the valuables on place being removed by those who took the body away?

(A) Those that were responsible for the taking of the body from material experiences, as has been visioned by those close to thee, also took the bond box away.

Reading 1349-1
25-Year-Old Male, Company Vice President and General Manager

(Q) Is there a way to work out my present economic depression?

(A) Only in the ways and manners as we find that have been indicated. The present associations seem to be hopeless, unless there may be the bringing of other interests—which should have been considered, as indicated, in the beginning. But make the associations rather with those types of activity as indicated, if these are appealing, or if these answer to that something within that seeks expression; and we will find the greater economic change, the greater satisfaction in every way and manner.

Reading 2560-1
65-Year-Old Female

Hence we may oft find the entity in the present able to discuss first principles with those who may be so minded as to turn to such, knowing scarcely from whence such judgments come.

The name then was Anna Divoak. It may be said that the entity gained materially, mentally, and in the latter portion gained much spiritually. For, that of freedom became a part of the entity's experience.

Thus the present ability to "give and take" and yet not be moved by reverses or abundance—and here most individuals fail. They may struggle and gain through adversity, but in prosperity fail to give proper values to spiritual, mental and material things.

Before that the entity was in the Norse land, when there was the breaking up of many of the traditions of those hardy peoples; when they entered into the Hun land and in the eastern portion of what is now known as France and those portions.

There the entity was in the opposite sex, and a leader, a ruler, a director in the affairs of the people as well as in the principles under which varied groups and various states of activity were formulated.

Again we see those principles innate in the present experience of the entity; its abilities to pass judgments upon or to draw upon rules of order and the regulating influences in the experiences of groups to which the entity may belong or in which it may be associated or affiliated.

Thus we find those principles because of which the entity has at times been termed, "You have the mind of a business man." These are innate and manifested, dependent upon the abilities of the entity to coordinate circumstance with its ideals in every phase of relationship.

Reading 531–3
40-Year-Old Male, Salesman

Look into the hearts of those that apparently are successful in material things, and unless such successes are founded in the spirit of justice, mercy, love and long-suffering and brotherly kindness, they must fade and fall away. Yet, if they are builded in these things that are the fruits of the spirit, they will grow and blossom as the Rose of Sharon; and ever will thyself in the spirit of thy angel that stands before His face find *pleasure* and grace and mercy in the eyes and heart of thine Maker.

Reading 2540–1
24-Year-Old Female, Model and Showgirl

When fear of the future occurs, or fear of the past, or fear of what others will say—put all such away with this prayer—not merely by mouth, not merely by thought, but in body, in mind and in soul say:

"Here am I, Lord—Thine! Keep me in the way Thou would have me go, rather than in that I may choose."

Reading 1856–1
16-Year-Old Male, Student

Of thyself alone little may be accomplished that is of lasting worth, yet much may be done in a material way to give or bring satisfaction, or gratification, to thy material desires. But these are of the earth-earthy.

Then, let thy life be so lived that the *material* successes come as a result of a clean, conscientious, consistent abiding in the faith, the promise from *Him* that ye are His son.

For the earth is the Lord's, and the fullness thereof. The silver, the gold is his; and the cattle, the grain upon a thousand hills are but as the workmanship of His hand. And He witholds no good things from those who abide wholly within Him and His promises.

Reading 1828–1
20-Year-Old Female, Freelance Artist

Let thy purposes then be grounded in spiritual things. Faint not at material disturbances. For the earth is the Lord's. Art thou His also?

The silver and the gold are his. Art thou acting in the manner and way in which He may entrust thee with such for the glorifying of His purposes? Or are ye inclined to glorify thy own?

Let not thy right hand know what thy left hand doeth, when ye come to say hard things against *anyone*, or when ye nourish those that are sad or discouraged. Not for thine own praise, but that ye may indeed know he even that giveth the cup of water in His Name shall not lose his reward.

Ready for questions.

(Q) What outlets are best suited to my talents?

(A) As indicated—in commercial art.

(Q) What does the immediate future promise along work lines?
(A) That in keeping with the sincere effort put forth.

(Q) Is my present business set-up advantageous to progress?
(A) It may be made either good or bad. If it is of self and self's purposes alone, it may be stalemated. If it is for the creative, for the beauty in same that may be enjoyed by the many, it is a constant growth.

(Q) Would marriage be an aid or a hindrance at this time?
(A) A hindrance—for at least six, seven, eight years.

(Q) Will I be capable of making happy the person I desire at present for a life partner?
(A) This must be a fifty–fifty proposition. But there will come another!

Reading 1716–1
63-Year–Old Female, Widow

(Q) What can I do to support myself, and where?
(A) Write—*wherever* you are—*write* of the introspection, and introspective experiences of self through the various spheres; as in meditation, in quiet, may the entity give much to others, and much that will come to self may bring in that of this world's goods as will care for *many*.

Reading 1597–1
31-Year–Old Male, Advertising Writer

Things pertaining to the arts of every nature; whether the workings in brass or in iron, or in carvings as of ivory, or in those things pertaining to such—all of these would be fields or channels through which material *expression* might be given of that which is innate.

But the purposes of same would be not merely for the material gains that come from same, but the material *gains* would come from same by that which is brought into the hearts and minds and experiences of those who behold same!

Hence in those fields in which these things and these characters may be presented for the edification, and for the knowledge, and for the teaching of the young or old, or all, are the fields through which the greater active service may be had.

Yet with it all, study to show thyself approved unto that consciousness, that God within; rightly dividing—and divining—the words of truth; keeping self from those questionings within thy own conscience—or, as He put it, unspotted from the world.

Reading 1120–1
29-Year-Old Male
Ready for questions.

(Q) During the next five years, what will be the predominating influences of my life?

(A) Depends upon what may be chosen as the activities. For, as indicated, first there should be the establishing of the home. Then there is to be set in the spiritual realm that which is to be its criterion, its measuring stick, its ideal. Then, these once set, show forth in thy material associations, in thy mental abilities, that the spirit of truth, of justice, of mercy, is *thy* guide.

(Q) What financial remuneration can I look forward to in the next five years?

(A) Sufficient to meet the needs, and to store that necessary for the development further. For, as ye use that today in hand as constructive forces in thy experience, whether it be of the spiritual, the mental or the material (for they build as one), then more is added.

(Q) In what way can I best develop myself mentally and spiritually?

(A) As indicated, by budgeting thy time.

Reading 165–10
52-Year-Old Male, Engineer, Manufacturer, Educator
(Q) Is the plan a good one to hold first meeting of the "Holdings Company for Health Room Experimentations" in N.Y., August 19th?

(A) Very good. The sooner the better—for, through some of the channels, many of the conditions as have been asked concerning may be worked out, as has been intimated or given—for these, as has been intimated and given, are of a far-reaching nature, and the associations can be MADE helpful, beneficial, in many various channels. That which can be helpful can also be detrimental. There has been the outline of policies, character of policies, as should ever determine those that would seek or would use, or would apply information as may be given from, through, by, or of such sources as these. They, the sources, [psychic sources] have their natural laws, just as others and to become compatible with, and useful to, an individual must be applied in that way and manner, or they may turn as a boomerang to one using or attempting to use such. These are the sources from which that is meant to be helpful, mindful, of the other fellow—and not of a purely selfish motive can one expect to gain thereby. Let this, then, be a means of self's development, in being of aid, assistance and helpfulness to the other fellow, and the position, the moneys, the bigness will be the result. Seeking for that as the result—yes …

Reading 137–7
26–Year–Old Male, Stockbroker

(Q) How can he put his finances in such a condition as to permit him to concentrate to his greatest possibility on his psychic development?

(A) Be not dismayed, for the development in psychic forces must manifest in and through the present conditions, and conditions physical, financial, must of necessity be one and a part of the development. As is given in this: In whatsoever state one finds (as he has found himself) oneself, make self content; not satisfied, but content, ever working toward that oneness of mind (of body, of will, with the development), or universal, or psychic forces. Do not war against these conditions. Make of conditions the stepping–stones to the development necessary to meet the daily needs in physical, in mental, in financial.

Reading 3063–1
56–Year–Old Male, Investment Counselor

Think not that, because they may apparently apply only to the mediocre mind, or to those that are of or in a certain faith, that they do not apply to thee. But know that the truth is applicable in every experience of the entity's life, whether as a shoestring vendor or a seller of such, or a director of some great financial institution, or even a leader or ruler over many peoples.

For, the same tenet that applies in one is true in the other. For he that would declare, "If I were so and so, how charitable I would be," or "If I were in this or that position what an effort I would make to magnify this or that," only attempts—in saying such—to give others a high opinion of self, and yet is not fooling even himself or anyone else! For if you give not when you have not even sufficient, though you were blessed with many millions, very possibly you would be much more stingy than you are now—and much harder to get along with—though you declare you wouldn't be!

In analyzing the urges latent and manifested, we would magnify the virtues and minimize the faults. This is the first lesson ye should learn: There is so much good in the worst of us, and so much bad in the best of us, it doesn't behoove any of us to speak evil of the rest of us. This is a universal law, and until one begins to make application of same, one may not go very far in spiritual or soul development.

Reading 3018-1
34-Year-Old Male, Machinist, Foreman

(Q) *Through what channels, and just what contacts should I make, to become affiliated with the organization referred to?*

(A) As indicated, make preparations, make a study in the present, for machinery and its activity as related to mining.

Know and understand the interest of such, the steel and its preparations in the various forms. Then make application to and through those channels for such.

(Q) *Why have I seemed to be unsuccessful in my work, or in any enterprise that comes my way?*

(A) As indicated, the lack of self-confidence. And the lack of self-confidence is the lack of surety. Make the surety in that which is eternal.

Reading 239-1
61-Year-Old Male, Artist

(Q) *What are the prospects for Eyescopes, Inc.?*

(A) This product, as is seen in the present conditions, is a sales proposition, and this, with many other of the holdings of the body, should be combined in or under one operative head for the handling or the distribution of such products. That is, these, as seen, have certain royalty and certain patent rights, as do other operatives that the body [239] is interested in. Get these combined under one sales organization, and through same *all* of these may be made *remunerative* to all concerned. But well

here may it be given this body, as long as there is held the consciousness of money and money power alone in the forefront of the body's
endeavors, these will only be ordinary in returns from same. Have, set,
make for self a goal to which the body would work to accomplish a
definite thing in this experience, and not be just mediocre in the ideas,
or most of all the ideas of that that is attempting to be accomplished
other than just making money. Money takes wings easily. The body
mentally, [239], has *abilities*—many abilities—many abilities, in that the
body may accomplish—may accomplish in most any direction that it
desires, but fear so often takes hold, loss of confidence in others so often
pushed forward, that the hindrances are ever apparent. Then, in
Eyescopes, in those other interests in which the body has interests—
combine these—force the combination through, and holdings under one
common head, share with others in that in which the entity holds a
portion of that as is being accomplished through these, and we will
find—with the right intent and purpose—*much* may be made of these,
for they have their place and may be made useful in same. *Do* that.

Reading 2934-1
42-Year-Old Female, Secretary

(*Q*) *Can we together fulfil our desire of being channels for welfare to those with
whom we associate, doing greater work than each one of us could do singly?*

(A) Much greater, and across the border—north, not south.

(*Q*) *Is there anything specific I should do to bring about more economic security
and greater serenity, than giving what present moral support I can from this great
distance, to said James [...].*

(A) This is the greater support, in the meditation and prayer that may
strengthen—"As ye give, ye receive."

Reading 5347-2
35-Year-Old Male, Navy Radio Technician

Let, then, rather thy prayer be, yea, thy tenet, thy sincere self, "Lord,
lead thou the way, and let my going in, my coming out, my dealing
daily with my fellow man, be in keeping with that thou would have me
do," and you will keep on an even keel.

For ye have a way with others! Use it for His glory, not for thine own satisfaction only. For ye will make money, but money and fame easily take wings and fly away, unless ye are in partners with thy Maker.

The appearances in the earth have much more to do with thy personality and individuality than the sojourns in the realms between same. Thus ye are tended towards judgments by material standards and these are false standards. Take warning! For what mattereth it to a man that He gain the whole world, yet lose his own soul? Know there is nothing that may separate thee from the love of GOD but thine own self. No urge, no activity may break thy will, if ye will ask, as indicated, "Lord, be Thou the guide."

Reading 5272–1
30-Year-Old Male, U.S. Army Lieutenant

(Q) *What geographic location would be best?*

(A) As indicated, the southern portions of Europe or in North Africa.

(Q) *What inhibitions, if any, are present?*

(A) The tendency to spend more than ye earn. Be mindful of this!

(Q) *Can you suggest any person or organization that I should contact?*

(A) This should begin by studying languages and whatever groups or whatever manners. The best way is to study them by radio or phonograph.

(Q) *In what way will my wife be able to contribute?*

(A) As the wife was the daughter in the experience before this, she may contribute much, dependent upon the unity of the activity.

Reading 4090–1
Adult Male

(Q) *How shall this body overcome other difficulties he has had, Mr. Cayce?*

(A) Difficulties are given to be overcome. What is not of his own making, forget. Those of his own making, study them and try correct them.

(Q) *What are the weak points of this body, Mr. Cayce?*

(A) Indecision and selfishness, these are his weak points.

(Q) *Will financial conditions soon begin to improve?*

(A) With labor, yes; without labor, no.

(Q) *Does this body affect the forces favorably?*

(A) Unless it changes it would not, but it is capable of changing. The change should first be worked on the physical body, they can be changed and they should be; there is destruction in the physical body for itself unless the forces are changed for the better.

Reading 4084–1
14–Year–Old Male, Student

Venus gives appreciation of music, lectures on music and its attunement to the harmony it brings into the experience. The entity may become a critic of music, art or literature. All of these should be parts of the entity's preparation for its contribution to the making of the world and its environs a better place, because of the efforts of the entity. The efforts should never be expended purely for mercenary reasons, but the pecuniary gains should come as a result of the abilities and desires of the entity being used in that direction of contributing helpful forces. For these would of themselves bring the material things, just as virtue in itself brings its own reward…

(Q) *Which of my aptitudes, active or latent, shall I follow for the greatest success in adult life, financially?*

(A) Forget the financial angle and consider rather that outlet for the greatest contribution the entity may make to the making of the world a better place in which to live. Let the financial gain be a result of the abilities being used rather as the lecturer or critic.

Reading 3663–1
63–Year–Old Male

(Q) *What proportion of net earnings from any endeavors should I give to the Association for Research and Enlightenment, or church?*

(A) These should be chosen by the entity. for what is to be given in this or that direction for any purpose shall be prompted by the real heart of the individual, and not by even a suggestion from others.

Reading 3509–1
29–Year–Old Female, Motion Picture Secretary

Turn again first to those principles latent deep within thee in spiritual things. First find thyself. Analyze the ideals. Know in what direction ye would go, and with what spirit thy purposes are prompted—that it may bring fame or fortune or that ye may be highly spoken of in certain circles, that ye may gratify thy own vanity, that ye may add to those things? Do ye say to thyself, "Yes, when I have attained, I will give this or that or the other"? If you don't give yourself, though you make but fifty cents a day—though you feel that you would give so bountifully if you were a millionaire, you wouldn't do a thing if you had a couple of million! This is fooling yourself! Ye are fooling yourself in planning what ye would do when ye attain. Do it now! Begin! For the individual soul-entity grows in grace. You don't hop off a ladder up on the upper boughs! You grow, you climb up! You *grow* to that. It unfolds, it develops with the character, with the purpose, with the ideal of the entity.

Reading 281–5
Prayer Group Reading

(Q) *Please give the healing group an affirmation that may be used in blessings our offerings as they are received?*

(A) May this be used in the manner as may be directed by Him, the Giver of all gifts.

Reading 281–13
Prayer Group Reading

Be not as the Pharisees, who love to be seen of men, who make long dissertation or prayer to be heard of men. They *immediately* have their reward in the physical–mental mind.

Be rather as he that entered the temple and not so much as lifting his eyes, smote his breast and said, "God be merciful to me a sinner!"

Which man was justified, this man or he that stood to be seen of men and thanked God he was not as other men, that he paid his tithes, that he did the services required in the temple, that he stood in awe of no one, he was not even as this heathen who in an uncouth manner, not with washed hands, not with shaven face attempted to reach the throne of grace?

Here we have drawn for us a comparison in prayer: That which may be the pouring out of the personality of the individual, or a group who enter in for the purpose of either outward show to be seen of men; or that enter in even as in the closet of one's inner self and pours out self that the inner man may be filled with the Spirit of the Father in His merciful kindness to men.

Now draw the comparisons for meditation: Meditation, then, is prayer, but is prayer from *within* the *inner* self, and partakes not only of the physical inner man but the soul that is aroused by the spirit of man from within.

Reading 262–125
Study Group Reading

In that outline first indicated here, who is to judge as to what is sin and what is righteousness for the individual? As we remember, as has oft been given, "Study to show *thyself* approved unto God, a workman not ashamed."

Here we find much that may need analyzing, looking into, in our own individual experiences. Do we, as children of God, as seekers after God, have firsthand knowledge? or do we accept only that others have told us? Do we condemn any? Do we know, or is it only self-righteousness that speaks?

Are we living that life that exceeds the righteousness of the Pharisee; who gave his tithes, who attended to the offices of his position, who met regularly in those capacities for activity of guidance, teaching and directing of others? Yet, what lacked he? Did he teach the letter of the law and forget the spirit of same?

Let each ask self, "Do I manifest—in speech, in activity—that I sincerely believe? Do I give credit to the spirit where credit is due? Do I adhere to the spirit of brotherly love? Do I sow the seeds of kindness with a kindly feeling, or with merely a sense of duty? Do I have long-suffering because I just can't help myself, or because I am willing that God—through His Son, through the Master of masters, show me the way? Is my life, my speech, my activity among others, in keeping with such righteousness as *He*—the righteous Master—taught?"

He said, "Be ye *perfect*, even as my Father in heaven is perfect." Would we modify that? Would we say that such is only to be sought, to be tried for, to be desired in the experience, and is not attainable here or now, under the present environs, the present hates, the present fears?

Was *He* unreasonable? Was He kind to those who despitefully used Him? Did His righteousness come as boastings of what His abilities were, of what He knew within Himself; or rather under those conditions wherein He came unto His own and His own received Him not, yet He condemned none?

Reading 451-1
21-Year-Old Female, Art Student

(Q) *Name a place of employment best suited for entity's vibrations.*

(A) Those as would have to do either with wall papers that are of pattern making, or of perfume manufactures. These, as we find, are—then—either in Paris, or in portions of New Jersey.

(Q) *How much should she give of her earning capacity to charity?*

(A) Ten percent, as all should. [Tithing—Deut. 12:6; Heb. 7:2]

(Q) *What mental attitude should be assumed toward people who upset her vibrations?*

(A) Keep that as has been given, as respecting the attitude the entity should assume; knowing that the desires are of a threefold nature. Spiritual, physical, and material. Two are the gratifications of self. The other is the keeping of that divine force that is within. The mental is the builder, for thoughts are deeds—they may become crimes or they may become miracles, whether guided by the spirit of truth, or as to the gratification of self's own interests. In the same attitude as one would be dealt to, so keep that attitude—as to how one, whether an enemy, a friend, a foe, or what not—"As ye would that men should do to you, do ye even so to them." So fulfil the law of love, that—"As a man soweth, so shall he reap." As an attitude is held towards another, that is gradually builded within self—and one may hold self aloof from another until there becomes such a barrier, even through those conditions of thought, as may *separate* one from another—but it may be builded in love, builded in that of preferring one above another, preferring another before self. Mind not high things, but condescend to those of low estate, for even as *He* gave, so may *we* in the activities of our daily life, though we may be attuned to that position wherein art becomes a portion of self, and one becomes attuned to everything in nature; yet nature *is* a manifestation of every form that we may see of the divine, making force manifest of the Creative Energy; for "In Him we live and move and have our being," and to make, or to hold one thing above another is to be idol worshipers.

Reading 1759–1
41–Year–Old Male

Then, let thy well [wellspring? Pr. 16:22; 18:4] be renewed within thee, that ye may show forth in the days of thy awareness as to thy relationship to thy brother, that ye take thought of him in that as ye would have men do to you, ye do even so to them.

For this experience is for thy own holiness, if ye will but look to Him. For God hath not willed that any soul should be in shame, in discouragement, bound with the fetters of circumstance or of obligation, but would have thee *free*—as He hath given thee thine *own* will—yea, thine own soul, and said "If ye will be my son, I will be thy God."

Hast thou drawn away? Hast thou neglected thy sonship, thy kinship with thy Maker?

Have ye looked upon the circumstances of others and envied them, or coveted their position or their place? Then, know ye have brought condemnation to thine own self!

Reading 1647–1
5–Month–Old Male

The material successes are not always real success; neither are those of such a nature as to not make the material life a practical experience a success.

Reading 1599–1
54–Year–Old Female

(Q) *What should the entity do for greater activity and expression?*

(A) Such should be the outgrowth of the purposes, rather than to be set as rules or laws. For as all phases of the human experience and relations are the outgrowth of what ye do *about* thy opportunities, then ye *grow* to these; and they are not laid down by rules that ye are to do this or to do that! But what is thy mission? What do ye desire to do? What manner of life do ye live?

Life itself is the expression of the Creative Force. That is eternity. What are ye doing about same!

(Q) *Would it be wise to marry again?*

(A) Again it must be the choice within self. If it is for self-gratification, for self-security, know that they who would have life must give it! they who would be secured must make security for others, in the mental and spiritual sense! For these are the outgrowth, not things to be sought within themselves alone!

Reading 2029–1
54-Year-Old Female

(Q) *What should be my life work?*

(A) As indicated—aiding others to better understand themselves and their relationship to Creative Forces as manifest in their lives—or a knowledge of God.

(Q) *Am I giving satisfactory service to others in Eastern Star and Daughters of the Nile organizations, sufficient to warrant promotion to the highest office in those groups?*

(A) As has been indicated, there is, there has been advancement in this experience—and the service and the abilities warrant the advancement.

(Q) *Where and how may I learn to heal mental and physical ills?*

(A) Within self—by the study of vibration as related to human emotion—or in those studies also as combined or compared with the teachings of the Teacher of teachers.

(Q) *Where can I get concrete guidance besides from the inner voice?*

(A) Seek not other than that of His meeting thee within thine own temple. For beside Him there is none other. Know, as He gave, they that climb up some other way are robbers.

Then, listen—listen to that voice within. Prepare thyself, consecrate thyself, purify thy body, thy mind, in much the same manner as did those of old who were, or would be, the priests and priestesses to Jehovah. And then, open thy heart and thy mind to those promises; surrounding thyself with the consciousness of the Christ love. And He stands and knocks. Will ye entertain Him?

Then, do not entertain others . . .

(Q) *What should I do to become financially secure?*

(A) Be secure rather in the spiritual and mental self, and know that the supply is from Him—and it will be sufficient.

(Q) Is there any danger about which I should be forewarned?

(A) The development of self forewarns the entity, as has been experienced in more than one instance. Hence these are rather of such a nature that they are nil in the experience of the entity.

(Q) Is there any advice further I need?

(A) As has been indicated, much might be said as to the symbols and those influences—but apply that which has been indicated, looking within self more and more; and we will find more peace, more harmony, more understanding.

Reading 5605–1
Adult Female

(Q) What are her future financial prospects, Mr. Cayce?

(A) With a good physical body the development financially will be wonderful. Give to others and returns will be commensurate with what she will give to them. The choosing of stations of others' lives and as to what they are best fitted for, the designation of this body to the other is for those that can chose between the right and wrong, those that it would benefit, those that are real and those that are covered with sham. [They] will present themselves to this body in time.

(Q) How long before this will be realized?

(A) When the body is physically fit which should not be very far if followed as we have outlined.

Reading 1438–3
78–Year–Old Female

(Q) Will my son be able to find a job?

(A) That depends upon the application of the son; and much of the attitude of self as in relationships to same.

For these are ever the laws of cause and effect, the laws of supply and demand, the laws of the activities of associations of individuals either acting from the angle of service for service, or service through ingratiation or whatnot.

These are contingent upon applications of the individual's abilities in directions of associations with others. These then become dependent. Possible, but whether the application is to be made depends upon the individual.

(Q) Will there be advisable or a desirable development at ... [my estate in N.Y.] next spring?

(A) This again is contingent upon the activities of those that have indicated their desire to apply self in the direction of carrying forward the policies and activities that have been considered.

As we find, if agreements are reached with those who have *considered* the activities, *and* their associates, there will be developments worthwhile.

Reading 520–1
30–Year–Old Male, Salesman

(Q) Exactly what is the entity's proper sphere of activity?

(A) Just given as for the development of self. In that of a writer, as respecting those conditions that change the *thought* of people as applies to individuals, groups, *masses*, classes.

(Q) Can this be applied in business?

(A) Can't be applied much any other way!

(Q) To what business?

(A) *Any* business.

(Q) How much money must the entity accumulate to enable him to comfortably provide for his family—etc?

(A) Use that thou hast in hand! and he that will not contribute to the humanitarian interest with one *penny* above the needed from day to day, will *not* contribute were there *millions* at hand! *This* a truth.

Reading 594–1
36–Year–Old Female, Restaurant Owner

(Q) What specifically am I best fitted to do?

(A) To instruct or to influence others as to their mode of carriage, and their abilities as to that of voice or acting.

(Q) When will I enter into my true life's work?

(A) When there has been the decision in self as to the way, the manner in which self may apply self in the field in which it desires to expend self.

As *we* find, the body is already entering into what may be said to be its true life work.

(Q) What is my work in the Study Group work?

(A) In making the material application of the truths as set forth in those that may be applied in the higher *modes* of expression in the lives of others; that is, as the truths apply to the emotions of the body in the expressing of same, see?

(Q) What is my special work in the Ass'n for Research & Enlightenment?

(A) This may be an aid to the body, as the body may be an aid to the Association; in enlightening others as to the truths that may be gained by the contact with that the Association has to give out. Hence well that the entity, the body, the mind, acquaint self the more fully with those truths and to the extent that these may influence the lives of others.

(Q) Have I known by husband [2516] in former incarnations; if so where and under what conditions?

(A) The husband was that one who kept the first theatre, and what is now called restaurant, in what is now Athens, Greece. Again he was known in those periods when the associations were as the *family* relations; being as a brother, but the one who was the husband at that time went off and left the body!

(Q) Is there any advice that will be given us that will help us to make a better living?

(A) In making application of those abilities in the associations and relationships respecting those things pertaining to what is called the *living*, or the commercial activities, set self in those ideas or plans whereby not only food is to be given for the body but also for the mind and soul of those whom the body contacts, and there will grow soon out of same that which will make for greater contentment and greater *blessings* to self and to others. For, as one sows—in body, in mind—so does one reap.

(Q) Have we been wise in taking over the Southland dining room to be run in connection with the Ragged Robin Coffee Shop?

(A) If they are made as coordinating factors, it may be well. If they are to be kept so entirely separate as to be a drain one upon the other, not so good. Let this be a little more explicit: Where the efforts are so used that they are to be independent one of another, they become a stumbling-block one for another, see?

(Q) *How may we be able to meet our obligations that we may be happier in our work?*

(A) Apply those things. Advertise more, and keep the place for the activities of the individuals in accord with that advertised.

Reading 705-2
Study Group Reading

(Q) *[683]: To bring a desired thing or condition into manifestation, is it advisable to visualize it by making a picture or just to hold the idea in prayer and let God produce it in His own way without our making a pattern?*

(A) The pattern is given thee in the mount. The mount is within thine inner self. To visualize by picturizing is to *become* idol worshipers. Is this pleasing, with thy conception of thy God that has given, "Have no other gods before me?" The God in self, the God of the universe, then, meets thee in thine inner self. Be patient, and leave it with Him. He knoweth that thou has need of before ye ask. Visualizing is telling Him how it must look when you have received it. Is that thy conception of an All-Wise, All-Merciful Creator? Then, let rather thy service ever be, "Not my will, O God, but Thine be done in me, through me." For all is His. Then, think like it—and, most of all, act like it is.

.

EDGAR CAYCE'S A.R.E.

What Is A.R.E.?

The Association for Research and Enlightenment, Inc., (A.R.E.®) was founded in 1931 to research and make available information on psychic development, dreams, holistic health, meditation, and life after death. As an open-membership research organization, the A.R.E. continues to study and publish such information, to initiate research, and to promote conferences, distance learning, and regional events. Edgar Cayce, the most documented psychic of our time, was the moving force in the establishment of A.R.E.

Who Was Edgar Cayce?

Edgar Cayce (1877–1945) was born on a farm near Hopkinsville, Ky. He was an average individual in most respects. Yet, throughout his life, he manifested one of the most remarkable psychic talents of all time. As a young man, he found that he was able to enter into a self-induced trance state, which enabled him to place his mind in contact with an unlimited source of information. While asleep, he could answer questions or give accurate discourses on any topic. These discourses, more than 14,000 in number, were transcribed as he spoke and are called "readings."

Given the name and location of an individual anywhere in the world, he could correctly describe a person's condition and outline a regimen of treatment. The consistent accuracy of his diagnoses and the effectiveness of the treatments he prescribed made him a medical phenomenon, and he came to be called the "father of holistic medicine."

Eventually, the scope of Cayce's readings expanded to include such subjects as world religions, philosophy, psychology, parapsychology, dreams, history, the missing years of Jesus, ancient civilizations, soul growth, psychic development, prophecy, and reincarnation.

A.R.E. Membership

People from all walks of life have discovered meaningful and life-transforming insights through membership in A.R.E. To learn more about Edgar Cayce's A.R.E. and how membership in the A.R.E. can enhance your life, visit our Web site at EdgarCayce.org, or call us toll-free at 800-333-4499.

Edgar Cayce's A.R.E.
215 67th Street
Virginia Beach, VA 23451-2061

EDGARCAYCE.ORG